Max Landsberg is a board advisor and leadership coach. As a partner at McKinsey & Company, his responsibilities included helping consultants develop their coaching and other professional skills – and he developed and led one of the UK's first company-wide coaching programmes. He was also a partner at headhunters Heidrick & Struggles where he established a Leadership Consulting division and advised large organisations on leadership and succession issues. Now a senior partner at Korn Ferry, he specialises in CEO development and succession. He studied Physics at Cambridge, has an MBA from Stanford, and lives in London.

His books draw on more than thirty years of his counselling individuals, teams, and corporations; they have become bestsellers, available in fourteen languages.

Also by Max Landsberg

The Tao of Motivation

Inspire yourself and others. A guide to simple techniques and habits, to help you: Feel and picture the success you want; Tap into your personal energies; Build your confidence, step-by-step; and more.

The Tools of Leadership

How to build Vision, Inspiration and Momentum in the team you are leading or managing. Includes chapters on: Culture and Trust; Charisma and Power; Influence and Timing; and more.

The Call of the Mountains

Sights and inspirations from a journey of a thousand miles across Scotland's Munros – and how you too can find adventure.

THE **TAO** OF **COACHING**

Boost your effectiveness at work by inspiring and developing those around you

MAX LANDSBERG

P

PROFILE BOOKS

This paperback edition published in 2015 by
PROFILE BOOKS LTD
3 Holford Yard
Bevin Way
London WC1X 9HD
www.profilebooks.com

First published by HarperCollins in 1996

Copyright © Max Landsberg 1996, 2002, 2015

Printed and bound in Great Britain by CPI Group (UK) Ltd, Coydon, CR0 4YY

A CIP catalogue record for this book is available
from the British Library.

ISBN 978 1781253328
eISBN 978 1782831 839

Contents

To my father who was an excellent coach,
and to my mother, who remains one

Introduction

*How come whenever I ask for a pair of hands I get a whole
person instead?*   Henry Ford

*The meeting of two individuals is like the contact of two
chemical substances: if there is a reaction, both are transformed.*
                                                          C. G. Jung

Into this book I have packed all the best tips and techniques
for coaching that I have encountered during thirty years of
working with teams and individuals. In doing so, my aim is to help
you grow the skills of other people – whether you are a team leader
or a professional coach.

This is a slim volume. That is because to become a great coach
you need master only a few techniques, even though mastery
obviously requires practice. Each chapter therefore focuses on
a specific technique of coaching and, to help you practise, each
technique is also illustrated by an episode in the dramatic life of a
man called Alex.

The great advantage, when introducing a third edition, is that
you actually know roughly to whom you are talking! When this tool
kit was originally published in 1996 I thought it might interest a few
enlightened business leaders.

But history has proved me wrong: a) the number of enlightened leaders seems to be much greater than I had thought, b) many
people have found these techniques also help them talk better with
their customers (not just with their own teams), and c) this tool kit
seems to be relevant well beyond the mere corporate world – the
response I cherish most is from a parent who described how the
techniques had helped him coach his children.

As a result, this volume and its companions on Motivation and
Leadership have sold over 200,000 copies, and have been translated
into fourteen languages.

But I have made several substantial changes for this third edition.

Firstly, I have included two new chapters. While many aspects of effective coaching do not change much over time, and our hierarchy of needs remains broadly similar from year to year, there were two topics that I thought deserved more attention and a chapter each: the power of effective questions, and a deeper treatment of goal-setting.

Secondly, I have reviewed Alex's life history and modernised him where he, or the events that impinge on him, needed to be brought up to date

And finally, I have attempted to improve the quality of the prose, aiming to change for the better those paragraphs that had me and some other readers cringing.

Why coach?

So why all this interest in coaching? 'Selfishness as much as philanthropy' seems to be the surprising answer.

People who coach others reap many unexpected rewards. You do not just receive the philanthropic buzz of having 'helped someone to develop'. As a great coach you also:

- Create more time for yourself: having developed the skills of your people, you will be in a position to delegate more.
- Enjoy the fun of working with a band of colleagues who actually relish working with you!
- Achieve better results, as a team, more quickly.
- Build your interpersonal skills more broadly – which often means you become better at interacting with your customers, and even with your family and friends.

In other words, the selfish reasons to become a great coach are often just as powerful as the philanthropic reasons. This simple yet powerful observation came as a big surprise to me, as it has to others in the many workshops I have led.

Of course, this will come as no surprise if you are versed in the Law of Karma! This yin-yang of increasing your own effectiveness while helping others to develop is the reason why this book is called *The Tao of Coaching* – see Figure 1.

Back in the 1990s it was clear that the autocratic leader was facing extinction. This was as true for leaders of families as for leaders of teams and of businesses.

Now it is even clearer that a new breed of leader is called for: a breed with a broader repertoire of management styles – sometimes 'hands-on' and sometimes 'hands-off', as suits the occasion.

More practically, this new breed recognises that even the greatest leader cannot do the whole job unaided. Changes in the business world mean the boss can no longer second-guess the staff, no longer be omniscient enough to monitor everything, no longer omnipresent enough to take all corrective actions required. Yet, at the opposite extreme, the effectiveness of the purely 'empowering' manager has not been proven.

Thus the new leader has to delegate appropriately; requires a following of able apprentices; and is usually the person best placed to build the abilities, on the job, of those who report to him (or her).

This new-style leader also believes that 1) if you invest just ten minutes in coaching someone who reports to you, it will later save you an hour; and 2) you also help yourself when you help others to perform more strongly.

What is coaching, and how to master it?

What are the secrets of excellent coaching, and how might this book help you to acquire them? I have tried to summarise the essence of coaching in the following definition.

● Coaching aims to enhance the performance and learning ability of others.

Figure 1

The Tao of coaching

Increase *your* effectiveness as a leader

... by helping *others* to develop and grow

Typical beliefs of great coaches:

- You can't be a leader without a following
- The autocratic boss is facing extinction
- Investing ten minutes in coaching will save an hour
- How to win friends and influence people –
  become a great coach

- It involves giving feedback, but it also includes other techniques such as motivation and effective questioning. And for a manager-coach it includes recognising the coachee's readiness to undertake a particular task, in terms of both their will and skill.

- Overall, the coach is aiming for the coachee to help her- or himself. And it is a dynamic interaction – it does not rely on a one-way flow of telling or instruction.

- A glance at the contents page and the glossary of this book will show you in more detail the tool kit of the great coach. And after reading any of the self-contained chapters, you should be able to practise using a specific technique. Each chapter illustrates a coaching technique in action, and ends with a single-page summary of how to do it.

Alternatively, you may wish to read the book from cover to cover and follow the dramatic 'true-to-life' story of Alex's career with its ups and downs, as Alex is coached well and poorly, and as he tries his own hand at coaching others.

But I suggest you start by completing a brief self-appraisal (Appendix 1), and ask others to complete a copy for you if you feel up to it.

As times change ever more rapidly, it is ever easier for us to fulfil Andy Warhol's prediction that we will all be famous for fifteen minutes. But it is ever more difficult for us to be remembered for fifteen years.

Let your legacy be that you were an excellent coach, inspired many imitators, and many great-grand-imitators too.

Max Landsberg
January, 2015

Contemplating coaching at work

In which Alex examines whether his skills as a coach warrant his being elected to the Board

Alex wondered whether this was his last chance. Although he had been promoted into a senior management position, it had taken a year longer than he had expected. The question now was whether he would be elected to the Board of Directors – and what would happen to him if he failed. It was now or never, and it wouldn't be plain sailing. 'At least I've given it my best shot,' he thought. 'I might as well enjoy my vacation.'

Alex settled back into his chair beside the pool and gazed out over the Aegean, oblivious to the playful shrieks from the beach below. He tried to relax, but wished he'd arranged the vacation for two weeks later, after the Board back in London had made its decision.

He congratulated himself, however, on having found the one villa in which he could get phone reception. Perhaps he'd get a call after the Board meeting? He glanced nervously over his shoulder to check that no one had knocked the phone into the pool, unplugged the charger or otherwise tampered with it.

As if by telepathy, the phone rang. Was it for Alex? It was! Was it his assistant Julia back at the office? It was! Was he now a Director? 'I'm afraid they've had to delay the meeting until tomorrow – I thought I should let you know,' she apologised.

'No problem,' he said, cursing inaudibly. 'Please let me know if you hear anything.'

○◯○

He thought about last week's day trip to Delphi. What were the words carved above the gateway to the Oracle's chair, to prepare the ancient enquirers on their way to the prophet? That's it: 'Know thyself.'

'OK,' he resolved, 'half an hour of introspection, my own decision on whether I deserve to be a Director, and then unadulterated vacation.'

○◯○

The problem was in some senses straightforward. Alex knew that, on the plus side, he had led a major reorganisation, implemented a courageous acquisition and turned around a loss making subsidiary. The only minus – but it had been a major one – was that he had sometimes tended to use people, and a few had been left burnt-out. He had acquired a reputation as a 'people eater'; at one point it had reached a stage where no one really wanted to work for him, or with him.

Five years earlier, the Board might have overlooked this character flaw. But now the management skills and habits necessary for building people's abilities, for helping them to develop, for coaching them, had assumed far greater importance. A deficiency in this area would not go unnoticed.

Deep down, Alex recognised that this new emphasis on people development had been driven by several powerful forces which were now affecting most large companies. First had been a trend towards reducing the number of management levels in organisations' hierarchies – i.e., 'delayering'. Everyone was now working in cross functional teams for large proportions of their time. No longer were jobs and roles prescribed and static, so no longer could 'bosses' just go on telling 'subordinates' exactly what to do. Rather, the successful companies were now those in which people learnt new skills and habits from each other, and in which managers were also coaches.

Second, labour markets had changed. The most able people now knew that companies with a coaching culture did exist, and that it was much more fun and rewarding to work there. In addition, people were more mobile, and excellent organisations were focusing more on bringing out their people's potential in order to retain their best performers.

Third, business conditions, markets and technologies were now changing even more rapidly than in the past. This meant that companies could no longer rely on providing employees with a week or two of 'off site training courses' every year. Training now had to be continuous and 'on the job' – i.e., by coaching.

'Well,' mused Alex, 'am I good enough at this coaching stuff?' Intuitively he thought he was indeed now a good coach. He hadn't been a 'natural' at it when he had joined the company a few years ago, but he'd picked up a few good coaching habits along the way. These had helped him to become much more effective as a manager, so he had kept an eye open for more tips from coaches who were role models. He had also read a great book on the subject, and had put into practice many of its suggestions. His only problem had come about a year ago when pressures to achieve had caused him to slip back into some bad old habits, resulting in his failure to be elected a Director.

But he had decided to mend his ways, and people now wanted to work with him again. He even found that his personal relationships outside work had improved.

On balance, he was about to elect himself a Director ... To be absolutely certain of his decision, however, he decided to review his own 'moments of truth' in coaching during his time with the company. This would allow him to reach a well informed decision. It would also provide the basis for lending his weight to the company wide coaching programme. Great intentions and promises so often spawned as a supplication to the gods at times of crisis ...

With the benefit of hindsight, Alex began to review how much he'd learnt about coaching – not only from his own coaching practices as a senior manager, but also from his early experiences of having been coached by others.

He picked up the phone, tapped the recording app, and began to speak – recalling the lessons of his career since he'd first joined the company.

This is Alex's story ...

'Ludwig, are you deaf or what? If I've told you once, I've told you a thousand times, drop the music schmoozic and get a proper job ...'

Ask questions – don't just tell – when helping others to develop their skills

Asking versus telling

In which Alex learns that 'coaching by asking' is often more effective than 'coaching by telling'

Alex was tearing his hair out. He had just joined the company in the strategic planning department, and was halfway through his first project. He was used to gathering facts on market trends, and analysing lots of numbers, but he wasn't used to writing the succinct reports that seemed to be the norm in this, his new company. He had developed what he thought was a creative title page for his document: 'Acquisition in the ice cream market – cold logic or soft option?' But he was having real problems in structuring his thoughts for the main body of the report.

Unfortunately for Alex, it was while wrestling with this problem that his boss, Bob, dropped by on an unscheduled visit. Bob was unimpressed, 'you need to start with the main message,' Bob eventually explained, 'and then structure the supporting rationale – ideally into three points, because most audiences can easily assimilate three points – in one of two ways. Either use a grouping of parallel points, or use a logical flow of argument: statement, implication, resolution. I have to go to a meeting now, but let's meet up later to run through your draft.' Alex had been confused by this rapid set of instructions. They had not made much sense to him, and by the end of the afternoon had made little progress.

Alex wondered whether Sarah could help. As a senior marketing manager, she had been involved in recruiting Alex into the company, and he suspected that she had been influential in the decision to offer him the job. She and Alex had many things in common – they had been to the same business school, were both interested in direct marketing, and were both keen tennis players.

Sarah was sympathetic to Alex's plight in structuring the report. 'What's the most extreme statement you would feel comfortable making about this ice cream market?' she asked.

'Well, I'm not yet sure that we should actually enter the market, but it does look attractive,' he replied.

'And why does it look attractive?'

'Well, demand is rising, profit margins look sustainable, competition does not seem to be very intense, and prices have held up over the last five years.'

'I see,' she replied, 'and are any of these four points really different sides of the same coin?'

'I guess the point about pricing is really part of the statement about profit margins ... Hey ...,' he continued excitedly, 'I think I've got something on costs, too. So, I could say that the market is attractive because: (1) demand is rising; (2) profit margins are sustainable on both the price and cost side; and (3) competitors look likely to remain weak.'

'Anything else?' asked Sarah.

Alex chewed on his pen. As he had now developed a clearer structure for his report, he could more easily spot the gaps. 'The retailers,' he mumbled, 'I need to add something about their buying power ...'

'Thanks, Sarah. I think I can work on this structure. By the way, is this a grouping of reasons or a flow of argument? It looks like a grouping of reasons to me ...'

Alex was impressed by Sarah's approach. She had only spent a couple more minutes with him than Bob had, but she had really helped him structure the report – and she didn't even know anything about the ice cream market! She had just asked the right questions. He also felt more confident about drafting the next report, and thought he'd probably be able to learn a lot from working with Sarah in the future, if the opportunity arose.

Sarah, too, thought that the brief interaction had been worthwhile; she believed that Alex had a lot of raw talent, saw he learnt quickly and kept him in mind as someone she might co-opt to work with on a project in the future.

The coaching spectrum

Socrates saw himself as a 'midwife to understanding'. He believed that one can help people understand, but that one cannot make people understand – just as a midwife delivers the child, but does not give birth to it.

Similarly, the coach is a 'midwife to skill building', and is not typically a highly didactic teacher. The coach's most important decision is whether to instruct / suggest, or whether to ask a question – or indeed whether to use a style of interaction somewhere between these two extremes. You will face this decision in a wide variety of coaching situations – when deciding the topic on which to help the coachee, when providing feedback or when helping the coachee decide what to do next.

At work, many 'bosses' rely on telling others – directly or indirectly – what to do and (sometimes) how to do it. But, as a coach, it's important to have a broader range of approaches in your repertoire. The pivotal question is often more powerful than the instruction, as Socrates knew.

If there is one thing you do differently as a result of reading this book, simply try asking a few good questions where you might otherwise have issued an instruction or leapt into providing advice, as illustrated by Alex's story on the preceding pages.

The ask/tell repertoire

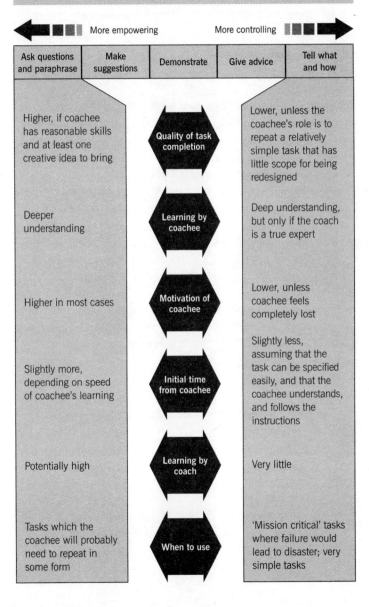

← ▰▰▰▰ More empowering   More controlling ▰▰▰ →

Ask questions and paraphrase	Make suggestions	Demonstrate	Give advice	Tell what and how
Higher, if coachee has reasonable skills and at least one creative idea to bring		Quality of task completion		Lower, unless the coachee's role is to repeat a relatively simple task that has little scope for being redesigned
Deeper understanding		Learning by coachee		Deep understanding, but only if the coach is a true expert
Higher in most cases		Motivation of coachee		Lower, unless coachee feels completely lost
Slightly more, depending on speed of coachee's learning		Initial time from coachee		Slightly less, assuming that the task can be specified easily, and that the coachee understands, and follows the instructions
Potentially high		Learning by coach		Very little
Tasks which the coachee will probably need to repeat in some form		When to use		'Mission critical' tasks where failure would lead to disaster; very simple tasks

'Oh, is that so? Well I'm the Top Banana, Head Honcho,
Big Cheese around here matey, and I say you're at
thirty thousand feet!'

Receiving feedback means active listening

3   Eliciting feedback

In which Alex learns how to elicit feedback from a colleague

Six months into his career with the company, Alex was feeling satisfied with his progress. He thought he understood how the company operated, and he had already made some substantial contributions. Although he didn't yet manage anyone else, he had practised his 'effective questioning' technique to good effect. On more than one occasion, he had constructively changed the course of a meeting through a well planted question – even though he already knew the answer.

But one thing still puzzled him. 'How on earth do I find out how well I'm doing here? No one ever tells me directly.'

The ice cream project had been moved to the back burner – a move which Alex thought had obvious dangers – and Alex was now working with Bob, his boss, on a project to streamline the company's production processes. He had been looking forward to the project, since he thought he had some particularly relevant skills to contribute. After all, he had studied engineering at university and had then worked as a production manager for two years before going to business school.

The project had started well. Alex had developed a good working relationship with Bob and felt that his work so far had been of real value. He had even had his first opportunity to make a full presentation to the divisional board.

But he realised that he was not getting much coaching or feedback. He had broached the subject tentatively with Bob a few times, including immediately after the last presentation. But Bob had merely responded that Alex seemed to be doing very well – and was, in fact, exceeding Bob's expectations.

Alex decided to seek out Sarah's advice again, and a few days later took the opportunity to sit next to her at lunch in the canteen. 'Sarah, I can't seem to get Bob to tell me properly how I'm performing. How do you manage to elicit helpful and constructive feedback?'

Her response was disarmingly simple. 'You have to ask, and you have to listen.'

Alex tried it later that week. 'Bob, could we have half an hour together, so that you could give me some feedback on how I've been doing for the last couple of months?'

'OK, Alex, but what would you like feedback on? I'm a bit surprised that you're asking for feedback, because I didn't really think that you wanted any.'

'What made you think that?' quizzed an astonished Alex.

'Well, you didn't take the initiative to talk through with me, when we started the project, the areas in which you wanted to build your skills. Also, the one time I did try to give you some feedback, you seemed very defensive.'

Alex did not want to become confrontational, but he did point out his two subsequent attempts to discuss his performance.

'Yes, I remember,' Bob replied, 'but both requests were in front of several other people. I got the impression that you just wanted some public acclaim. That said, I'm sorry for not following up later on. Anyway, what are the specific areas you'd like to have my feedback on?'

Alex was unsure. He had assumed that Bob, with his greater experience, would know exactly what to focus on. So they agreed to meet the next day, after Alex had thought about the areas in which he would most value some help.

They focused on Alex's strengths and weaknesses in delivering presentations, and had a highly productive half hour. Bob helped Alex to realise that he needed to establish eye contact with each person in the audience instead of with only one person, and that he needed to set the context more clearly at the beginning of his presentation.

As Alex left Bob's office he really did feel 'coached' – rather than 'evaluated'; Bob had been careful to discuss specific examples of what Alex had done, rather than talking about character 'traits'. Alex also had a clear plan of action.

'I suppose that obtaining feedback is as easy as "ask and listen",' thought Alex, 'although both you and your coach need to know enough about you to address the right topics, and you have to be careful to listen with an open mind, and without being defensive.'

Alex had jotted down the points on the following two pages for future reference, and had found them as helpful later on – when he had become a more senior manager – as they had been on that day. He also recalled a fragment of a poem which he had learnt by heart as a schoolboy:

> *If you can trust yourself when all men doubt you,*
> *But make allowance for their doubting too ...*
>
> Rudyard Kipling

Getting feedback

When was the last time that you received useful feedback? Probably too long ago: few people ever feel that they receive enough feedback. This is usually the lowest-rated item on any company-wide culture survey. And this is as true for older people as for younger ones; for the experienced as for the inexperienced; for the able as for the less able.

Although the primary focus of this book is on how to be a great coach, it is worth touching on the skill of being a great coachee. It's a valuable skill for the workplace, as well as for life in general. Managers and staff who fail to receive feedback (for whatever reason) disable an important self correcting mechanism and aid to personal productivity.

However, you cannot be a furtive coachee – you have to make it clear that you want feedback. And in asking for feedback you are asking someone to do you a favour (one that requires some courage on the coach's part), so you must also make the process as easy as possible for her/him. The facing page provides some suggestions.

Getting feedback – making it easy for the 'giver'

1 Choose the right 'coach' for the right topic, a coach whom you really trust. For example, you might want to choose different peers/subordinates/bosses/friends, depending on whether you feel you need feedback on:
  - Management style (choose someone whom you manage)
  - Presentation skills (alert a member of your audience)

2 Give your coach as much notice as possible, so that s/he can marshal relevant examples
  - Explain at the beginning of major pieces of work what you would like – e.g., feedback topics and the frequency of discussion
  - Remind your coach prior to the meeting – don't just 'turn up'

3 Take the initiative in building a trusting relationship
  - Volunteer your own perspective on areas in which you could improve (don't just try to highlight areas in which you are phenomenally excellent)
  - Explain what motivates you and what demotivates you; disclose other factors that might be relevant

4 Receive the feedback genuinely
  - Avoid being defensive (unless you never want feedback again!)
  - Follow what the coach says – show your genuine interest, summarise what you are learning, and ask for specific examples and explanations

5 Show your appreciation
  - Make real progress, and follow at least some of the advice
  - Let the coach know that s/he has made a difference; thank the coach

Exercise

Identify two people from whom you would value feedback this week, and ask for it.

'So just to recap, I like to be rubbed here, stroked there and massaged here, but don't ever fidget with this bit ...'

Coaching also benefits the coach

4 Correcting common coaching myths

*In which Alex reviews myths about coaching,
and comes to understand the selfish reasons for
becoming a great coach*

It had been three weeks since Alex had seen Sarah in the canteen, and he decided to drop by her office. 'Hi, Alex, I haven't seen you for a while, how are you?'

'Fine thanks,' he replied. 'Thanks for your advice on obtaining feedback. I had a really useful session with Bob.'

'That's great,' said Sarah, 'and I'm glad you're here because I was wondering if you could do me a favour. As you may know, the company's Human Resources Committee is taking a real interest in coaching. As part of the project I thought we should have an article on the topic in the company magazine. Perhaps a few key hints on how to do it, plus a section on why to do it. I've drafted a few pages, and I was hoping you'd be willing to review them and let me have your reaction.'

'I'd be happy to,' he replied, with a slightly confused expression. 'But isn't it fairly straightforward? I mean, don't people just provide feedback and coaching to help other people get better at their work?'

For the first time, Sarah looked at him condescendingly. 'Errr … Alex, there's slightly more to it than that! There are some unexpected angles for example. Like the selfish reasons to become a great coach, the fact that coaching is more than just giving feedback, and so on. Anyway, if you have a moment to read through my draft, I'd be very grateful.'

'*The Myths of Coaching* – seems like a good title,' he mumbled, as he left Sarah's office with the draft document.

THE MYTHS OF COACHING

There are five major myths surrounding what it takes to be a good coach. Here's an attempt to set the record straight.

by Sarah Jennings

Let's face it, coaching is not about being a 'nice guy'. It's about bringing the same structure and creativity to your interactions with colleagues as you bring to solving business problems.

But before we go any further in defining what it takes to be a good coach, let's address some of coaching's myths and realities.

Myth: We coach primarily to help others.

Reality: There are many tangible, selfish and acceptable reasons to become a great coach. In fact, good coaches find the personal payoffs so high that they rarely kick the habit. The following – listed in order of decreasing selfishness – is a sample of those payoffs:

- More time for yourself. You can either go home earlier or invest the time in higher quality work. While it's virtually impossible to prove, most great coaches believe that investing just ten minutes a day in coaching team mates typically generates at least 20 minutes of extra time per day for the coach.
- Better customer relations skills. By coaching colleagues you can hone the interpersonal skills which you need for building effective relations with customers and clients.
- Stronger organisation. If you plan on a long term career with the company, investing in the development of your colleagues is clearly worthwhile.
- More fun. You and others working in coaching-oriented teams tend to enjoy yourselves more.
- Stronger following. If you help others, they tend to help you. And if you aspire to be a leader, it's worth remembering that every leader needs a following.

Myth: Focus on the coachee.

Reality: Know thyself. Coaches don't focus exclusively on the coachee. In fact, great coaches have a high degree of self awareness. We all have the basic skills to coach; unfortunately, most of us have a few psychological blocks when it comes to applying those skills well and consistently. Great coaches know how to overcome their own blocks.

Myth: Coaching equals feedback.

Reality: There are many other important coaching tools and habits. While most people think that coaching is merely providing feedback and suggestion to coachees, the truth is that insightful feedback is only one tool in the coach's tool box. For example, good coaches typically master the art of effective questioning. Coachees can often learn more from a coach asking 'How well do you think you did; what might you do differently next time?', than from being told, 'Here's what you did wrong, and here's what to do next time'. There are also other tools, like the GROW approach and motivation techniques.

> Coachees can often learn more from a coach asking them how well they've performed a particular task than from being told, 'Here's what you did wrong, and here's what to do next time'

Myth: Coaching requires lots of time.

Reality: The best coaching comes in small doses. Many people believe that coaching comes in large quantums. But with á bit of practice, you don't need to change into a jogging suit every time you want to provide coaching. Small investments of time – as little as five minutes – can yield tangible increases in performance.

Myth: Coaching is about work.

Reality: Good coaching will spread to other areas of life. Those who develop their coaching skills at work usually find they are better able to help their friends, partners and children. In that respect, coaching is clearly a life skill.

Annual appraisals with Old 'Sparky' Watson tended to be a little traumatic ...

Guide – don't judge – when coaching

Giving feedback

*In which Alex delivers really effective feedback
for the first time*

Two weeks later, as Alex was reading Sarah's article on the myths of coaching in the company magazine, he thought about Gordon. Perhaps it was worth investing some time in coaching him.

Gordon, who had just graduated from university and had recently joined the company, was Alex's first direct report. The company had renewed its interest in the ice cream market and Alex, with Gordon's help, had been asked to figure out whether to acquire a large manufacturer of ice cream and frozen yoghurt: Cones-and-Tubs International.

Things had started well: they had assembled the relevant facts, interviewed some of the company's customers, and estimated how much Cones and Tubs was worth.

But soon Alex noticed that Gordon tended to disappear for long periods of time. He was undoubtedly working very hard, because whenever Alex managed to catch up with him, he always had reams of printout from his personal computer, with all sorts of weird and wonderful scenarios analysed in minute detail.

The problem was that Gordon had clearly gone off at a tangent on many occasions, and Alex felt sure this was because Gordon had not been paying attention in their periodic team meetings.

'Time for some feedback,' thought Alex, as he flicked through the booklet on giving constructive feedback which Sarah had given him.

The section on delivering feedback started with the usual caveats that there was more to coaching than just giving feedback; that feedback was, however, a critically important tool; and that it was difficult to generalise about how to do it well. 'Nevertheless,' it continued, 'in providing feedback, ensure you address three topics, with the acronym AID to help you remember them:

A   (Actions) The things that the coachee is doing well, or poorly, in the area under review

I   (Impact) The effect these actions are having

D   (Desired outcome) The ways in which the coachee could do things more effectively.'

Alex furtively closed the booklet as Gordon dropped by for the prearranged meeting. Alex started by reviewing the project's good progress to date, and congratulated Gordon on several aspects of his work so far. Then he continued, 'Gordon, I'd like to give you some feedback on your participation in our team meetings. Would you find that helpful?' Guardedly, Gordon nodded his assent.

'Well, I couldn't help noticing that you sometimes don't appear fully engaged in our team discussions.' Gordon twisted uneasily in his chair. 'For example, at the meeting yesterday you seemed to be doodling, and at times even staring out of the window. Would you say that was an accurate observation?' *[Description of actions]*

'I do sometimes feel a bit bored by the endless discussions,' Gordon replied. 'I suppose I'd just prefer to be getting on with the analysis.'

'OK, Gordon, but the problem this causes is that when the meeting has finished, and you go off to do your part of the work, you don't take account of changes in direction which everyone else has agreed to at the meeting. As a result, some of your work ends up being redundant, and you come across as rather arrogant, since it appears that you can't be bothered to listen to what your team-mates are saying.' *[Description of impact]*

'I recognise the first point about redundant work, but I didn't realise that I would seem arrogant,' replied Gordon, surprised.

'Let's see what we can do to address the situation,' suggested Alex. 'Do you have any ideas for getting more engaged in these meetings?' *[Discussion of desired outcome]*

Gordon didn't have any immediate ideas; it was, after all, his first

'real' job and he wasn't used to working in teams. So Alex continued,
'How about if we arrange for you to present your most recent work
at the beginning of each meeting? Or, better still, why don't we
expand your role on the project to include helping me in the overall
coordination? That way you would have a reason to keep track of
what's going on. Perhaps you could even summarise the agreed next
steps at the end of each meeting, before everyone leaves the room.'

This seemed to be a great idea. As Gordon left the office, Alex
reflected that, while this interaction had hardly been substantial
or interactive enough to be called 'coaching', it was nevertheless
constructive feedback.

Over the next few weeks Gordon became much more engaged
in proceedings, his team-mates stopped moaning about him, and
Alex found that he could delegate many of the project coordination
tasks to Gordon. Alex felt that the AID structure was both simple
and effective; he'd try to use it more often in the future.

Providing feedback

Providing feedback is one of the coach's most important skills. Narrowly defined, it means replaying to the coachee what s/he did in a specific situation. More broadly – and more usefully – defined, it includes highlighting the impact of what the coachee did. It also includes a discussion of what the coachee might do (even) better next time.

A few definitions:

- **Positive** feedback applies to situations where the coachee did a good job. It consists of simple praise, but is even more powerfully reinforcing when the coach specifically highlights why or how the coachee did a good job.

- **Constructive** feedback highlights how the coachee could do better next time. It needs to be delivered sensitively.
    - Use the AID mnemonics suggested earlier
    - When describing the coachee's actions, focus on specific observable facts ('In the last presentation you did not fully address some of the follow up questions'), not assumed traits ('you tend to be evasive')

- **Negative** feedback – i.e., merely replaying something that went wrong – is essentially destructive and is only used, usually by accident, to terminate friendships and marriages. It describes a perceived negative behaviour, without proposing a resolution ('You're always complaining').

To provide a factual context for your discussion of how your coachee performed, you can of course refer to notes which you took at the time, replay a video (if the coachee had agreed to being videoed) or ask a third party to comment.

Helpful hints for providing feedback

Bad feedback	Good feedback	Hallmarks of good feedback
Creates defensiveness and confrontation; focuses on blame	Creates trust and cooperation; focuses on improvements – possible or achieved	• Create a contract to discuss issues • Acknowledge coachee's feelings
Does not improve skill	Increases skill	• Focus on 'skills' not 'person' • Paint specific picture of desired skill • Suggest practical steps
Undermines confidence and self-esteem	Improves confidence in ability and potential	• Position as need to 'build' or 'demonstrate' vs. 'don't have' or 'must prove' • Balance negatives and positives; provide constructive actions
Leaves person guessing	Clarifies 'exactly where I stand' and 'what to do next'	• Verify with questions; ask for coachee's recap • Jointly arrive at plan
Leaves person feeling 'judged'	Leaves person feeling 'helped'	• Invite coachee to assess own performance first • Offer support for future

Exercise

Identify someone to whom you could provide useful feedback today (see Appendix 2, page 123), and follow through.

As he entered the back straight, Dave faced seven oncoming speedwalkers and the dawning realisation that he might have started off in the wrong direction.

Organise your coaching sessions well –
start in the correct direction

6 Structuring the coaching session: GROW

In which Alex encounters a master coach, and learns how to use the GROW* approach to structure coaching sessions

Alex jumped at the knock on his office door. 'How are you, Alex? I hear you are developing quite a reputation as a feedback merchant!'

It was Michael, the Chief Financial Officer of the company. He was senior to Alex, and a part time member of the multifunctional team – Project Quest – which Alex was leading to advise on the acquisition of Cones-and-Tubs International.

It was only 3 p.m., but Alex looked drained. 'I'm fine, thanks,' he replied without conviction.

'Alex, why not put the work down for half an hour? I can see that something is causing you a problem. Perhaps I can help.'

Alex accepted the offer gratefully. He had a particularly open relationship with Michael, who had been his informal mentor ever since their doubles victory in the company's annual tennis championship. 'I've been with the company for just over a year now, and I seem to be spending too much time running meetings. But I can't seem to get the discussions to make as much progress as I'd like. Perhaps I'm doing something wrong.'

'I can spare you 10 minutes,' Michael offered, 'why don't we see if we can figure out something to help you. But first, what is your goal – both regarding the management of meetings in general, and for our next 10 minutes together in particular? In other words, if I could grant you one wish for this session, what would it be?'

'I suppose it would be to have a brief checklist for how to manage meetings better.'

---

* Goal, Reality, Options, Wrap up – described on page 30

'And do you think we can accomplish that in the next 10 minutes?' Michael enquired.

'Let's give it a go, Michael, there's nothing to lose – I feel a lot better already, even thinking that there might be a solution.'

Michael asked Alex to be more specific about the reality of the situation. Just how did Alex know that there really was a problem? Were there particular situations in which he felt more, or less, able to manage the dynamics of meetings? What solutions had he tried so far? Of course, Michael had himself been a participant in many of the meetings which Alex had been chairing, and so was able to offer one or two of his own observations. However, he knew that it was Alex who had to do the diagnosis, if the ideas were to be useful.

Initially, Alex had felt that the main reason for his difficulty was a lack of ability in dealing with several awkward team members. But with Michael's guidance in thinking things through, he also realised that he didn't pay enough attention to planning the meetings in advance. 'So, Alex, which topic would you like to focus on – people or planning?'

'Let's talk about planning the meetings,' replied Alex. 'I'll need to put in some more thought before addressing the issue of how to interact with difficult team members.'

'OK, so let's focus on the options you have. What could you try? What have you seen work well in similar circumstances? Try to be radical.'

Alex reflected for a moment. 'I suppose I could put more thought into my preparations for the meeting.'

'How do you mean?' probed Michael, moving to the flipchart.

'Well, currently I prepare an agenda with a simple list of the topics for discussion. In future I could be more focused and actually list the specific issues we need to resolve. I could even list the team's hypotheses for resolving each issue – and circulate it prior to the meeting. That way we could really be focused.' Alex was beginning to look relieved, and he continued to brainstorm other ideas for better meeting preparation, with Michael throwing in occasional ideas of his own. (Michael even made a mental note of some of these ideas for his own subsequent use.)

'Time to wrap up,' said Michael eventually, glancing at his watch. 'Do you think you'll actually do any of this? What are the next steps? What support do you need, if any?'

Alex was sure that he would adopt the ideas they had just come up with – they would certainly be helpful. He also felt that he understood himself a little better, and would have more confidence to address similar issues in future. 'The only further favour I would ask, Michael, is that you give me a kick under the table at the next meeting if I haven't done any of that preparation in advance!'

'Goal, Reality, Options, Wrap up,' said Michael, as he was leaving Alex's office. 'That structure always seems to work if you want to have a really effective coaching session which goes beyond simply providing feedback. Google it one day.

'By the way, Alex, I really think we'll get approval for this ice cream acquisition. I've even heard your name mentioned as the person to run the post merger integration project – and that would probably mean a promotion. Of course, I'd be involved in the project too, as would Sarah Jennings on the marketing side. Do you know Sarah? I think you'd enjoy working with her.'

Structuring a coaching session – GROW

So, how do we actually structure a coaching session? The **GROW** (**G**oal, **R**eality, **O**ptions, **W**rap up) model is one of the most common coaching tools, widely used by many great coaches.

The framework provides a simple four step structure for a coaching session. During the first step of a session *[Goal]*, coach and coachee agree on a specific topic and objective for the discussion. During the second step *[Reality]*, both coach and coachee invite self assessment and offer specific examples to illustrate their points. They then move into the third step *[Options]*, where suggestions are offered and choices made. And finally *[Wrap up]*, the coach and coachee commit to action, define a timeframe for their objectives and identify how to overcome possible obstacles.

Here are a few tips for using this model:

- Use more 'ask' than 'tell'; elicit useful ideas from your coachee – don't just try to prove you are smart
- Think creatively – not just systematically, particularly in the Options and Wrap up steps
- Illustrate, and check understanding, throughout by using specific examples – from the coachee's and your own experiences
- If you have a follow up session, you can obviously lengthen or shorten each of the four steps as needed

The GROW model

- Agree topic for discussion
- Agree specific objective of session
- Set long-term aim if appropriate

- Invite self-assessment
- Offer specific examples of feedback
- Avoid or check assumptions
- Discard irrelevant history

- Commit to action
- Identify possible obstacles
- Make steps specific and define timing
- Agree support

- Cover the full range of options
- Invite suggestions from the coachee
- Offer suggestions carefully
- Ensure choices are made

Exercise

Find an opportunity to apply GROW this week. See Appendix 3 (page 124) for examples of questions to use.

Thompson and Maguire may not have seen eye to eye but they were the best forensic teams on the Force …

Great teams overcome differences in styles of working

Diagnosing individuals'
different styles

*In which Alex learns how to help two very
different people to work together*

A couple of weeks later, Alex was beginning to feel that his
life was more under control, thanks to Michael's advice
to use the GROW framework. But he still had problems with Tom
and Dick, the two members of the Project Quest team who were
always arguing.

Alex was unsure whether to just 'knock their heads together',
or whether a more probing approach would have greater and more
lasting value. At the end of a meeting with Michael, Alex sought his
advice on Tom and Dick. Michael did not beat about the bush.

'I've met them both a few times, Alex. I'll bet you that Tom's
an ENFP, and that Dick's an ISTJ.' Alex looked blank, so Michael
continued, 'Do you know anything about psychology?' Alex shook
his head, suddenly thinking that it was absurd that managers were
rarely taught much about what makes people tick.

'Well,' continued Michael, 'luckily, you don't need a degree in
psychology to be an effective manager and coach, but you do need
some way to figure out the different styles of interaction different
people prefer to use.

'Personally, I recommend something called the Myers-Briggs
Type Indicator. It sounds a bit of a mouthful, but it's really quite
simple. I'll give you a two minute description, but then I suggest you
download a guide to it.

'The Type Indicator provides a description of how people prefer
to operate in their daily lives. In meetings for example, you know
how some people like to stick rigidly to the agenda while others
prefer to leap from idea to idea? The first type of person could well
be an ISTJ, while the other might be an ENFP. If you know what
'type' a person is, it will help you a good deal in interacting with

them – and in helping them to work with each other.

'"So", I hear you ask, "what do these letters stand for?" The Indicator is based on four dimensions of how people prefer to operate. The first dimension relates to how they are *energised* – what turns them on. An Introvert (I) is energised by the inner world of thoughts and ideas, whereas an Extrovert (E) is energised by the outer world of people and things.

'The second dimension describes what the person prefers to pay *attention* to. A Senser (S) focuses on facts and the five senses, while, at the other end of the spectrum, an Intuiter (N) type focuses on what might be, and the sixth sense.

'The third dimension describes how the person prefers to *make decisions*. The Thinker (T) tends to use reason and logic, while the Feeler (F) tends to use values and subjective judgement.

'The final dimension describes the person's *overall approach to life* – with Judgers (J) preferring to be planned and organised, while Perceivers (P) prefer spontaneity and flexibility. If you take all the combinations, you'll find that these dimensions define 16 basic types of preference.'

Alex thought he understood. 'So, an ISTJ person [who prefers to be an Introvert and Senser and Thinker and Judger might think that an ENFP person [Extrovert, Intuiter, Feeler, Perceiver] was lax and disorganised, while the latter would think of the other as unimaginative and afraid of ever taking a leap into the dark? OK, I think I can see how I could use this, but how would I really know someone's "type"?'

'Sounds like an ISTJ kind of question, Alex! You can either have your team complete a standard questionnaire, if you think they're up to sharing the results. Otherwise, you'll just have to use your intuition. Why not have a chat with Tom and Dick separately about it. But if you do use the questionnaire, don't forget to read the caveats!'

Alex set off down the corridor to find Tom. He had always thought that Tom's corner cubicle was a disorganised mess, but now he understood a little better why this might not bother someone who valued flexibility, creativity and spontaneity.

After his discussions with both Tom and Dick, Alex concluded that the original diagnosis had been correct; far from there being some deep seated enmity between them, they just had very different preferred styles of working. He knew he had two options: either to reassign Tom and/or Dick to parts of the project in which they would not have to work together, or to address the issue head on. The latter approach had the advantages that *(1)* Tom and Dick would not have to get up to speed in new areas of work, and *(2)* the team could actually be more effective if these two team members could contribute their differing skills in a complementary way.

Alex opted for this latter course. In fact, he had everyone on the team, including himself, complete Type Indicator questionnaires, and share their results. Tom and Dick were wary of each other for a few days, but gradually settled down to productive collaboration, based on their better understanding of each other. Not surprisingly, Tom focused on coming up with creative ideas, and Dick on checking their practicality.

By the time Project Quest was completed, however, Alex was surprised to discover that Tom and Dick had shared their thoughts on what they had actually learnt from each other. Tom had mapped out the things he could do to be more organised when the occasion required it, and Dick had done likewise for creativity. Alex decided to encourage this type of mutual learning more actively in future.

Alex reflected on how valuable it was for team members, managers and coaches to have some simple model of how people interact, and to discuss this topic openly. He also realised how many misunderstandings derive from differences in style – rather than the most common interpretation: that the other party is dim witted or has poor intentions.

'But what's really powerful,' he thought, 'is when you have insights about individuals' styles, and combine them with the basic tools of coaching – asking effective questions, listening actively, providing clear feedback and using the GROW framework.'

Understanding preferred styles

There are many models for identifying and characterising the styles of interaction which we and others prefer to employ. A widely used approach is the Myers-Briggs Type Indicator (MBTI). It is based on the following four 'dimensions' of a person's preferred approach to life.

1   How you are energised (Extrovert vs. Introvert)

2   What you pay attention to (Sensing vs. Intuition)

3   How you make decisions (Thinking vs. Feeling)

4   How you live and work (Judgement vs. Perception)

To work effectively with someone, take their preferred style into account. For example, 'Judgement' types can become irritated by 'Perception' types who may stray from the agenda. Conversely, people strong on 'Perception' may see those who prefer 'Judgement' as unwilling to take the time to explore creative options.

The characteristics of each dimension are indicated opposite. For a more complete description, see *Please Understand Me* by David Keirsey and Marilyn Bates.

For more information about receiving a profile, contact:

⬤ Oxford Psychologist Press Ltd. http://www.opp.com (UK)

⬤ Consulting Psychologists Press, Inc. www.cpp.com (USA)

(The description of the MBTI has been modified and reproduced by special permission of the Publisher, Consulting Psychologists Press, Inc., Palo Alto, CA 94303 from *Introduction to Type* by Isabel Briggs Myers. Copyright 1993 by Consulting Psychologists Press. All rights reserved. Further reproduction is prohibited without the publisher's written consent.)

Myers-Briggs Type Indicator – key elements

1 *Energising (direction of energy)*   2 *Attending (perception)*

Extrovert (E)	Introvert (I)	Sensing (S)	Intuition (N)
• External	• Internal	• The 5 senses	• 6th sense
• Outside thrust	• Inside pull	• What is real	• What could be
• Blurt it out	• Keep it in	• Practical	• Theoretical
• Breadth	• Depth	• Present	• Future
• People, things	• Ideas, thoughts	• Facts	• Insights
• Interaction	• Concentration	• Using established	• Learning new
• Action	• Reflection	skills	skills
• Do think do	• Think to do	• Utility	• Novelty
		• Step by step	• Leap around

3 *Deciding (judgement)*   4 *Living (orientation to the outside world)*

Thinking (T)	Feeling (F)	Judgement (J)	Perception (P)
• Head	• Heart	• Planful	• Spontaneous
• Logical system	• Value system	• Regulate	• Flow
• Objective	• Subjective	• Control	• Adapt
• Justice	• Mercy	• Settled	• Tentative
• Critique	• Compliment	• Run one's life	• Let life happen
• Principles	• Harmony	• Set goals	• Get data
• Reason	• Empathy	• Decisive	• Open
• Firm but fair	• Compassionate	• Organised	• Flexible

Exercise

Think about yourself and someone with whom you have worked ineffectively – do you differ on any of these four dimensions? What might you have done to work better together? Consider arranging for you and your team to have your 'types' identified.

*Briggs thought he was the best syndicate accounts manager,
data analyst, economist, underwriter and plate spinner
Finklestein Hooch & Krupp had ever employed.*

Overcome your coaching blocks, or you
will never delegate

8 Finding and avoiding your coaching blocks

In which Alex forgets all his coaching lessons

The champagne corks popped as the deal was finally signed. By acquiring Cones-and-Tubs International, Alex's company had completed the largest take over in its history, and had become the world's largest maker of ice cream.

Alex had been appointed to lead Project Genesis, the integration programme, with a full time team of 12 people. He felt confident that he could perform, with promotion virtually guaranteed. 'Senior manager after only 18 months with the company – not bad!' he mused.

He set to work, laying out a punishing schedule for himself and the team. There was much to be done: defining the new management structure, confirming likely cost savings and synergies, reassuring key customers, and double checking the financial implications of the acquisition.

Bob, still Alex's boss, was becoming concerned. He had noticed that it was with a definite swagger that Alex had left his office with the good news that he had landed the project management role. And now Alex was being just that bit too eager.

Because the other team members were not available immediately, Alex had used the intervening time to plan the team's activities in great detail. 'Hmm ...' he thought, 'lots of data to be analysed on this project. I bet we'll also need to commission some market research, do some conjoint analysis to identify the relevant market segments, then we can figure out which marketing channels to use for each type of product in each geographic region ...'

Unfortunately, Alex was not really a marketing expert; yet by the time the people from the Marketing Department arrived on the team, they found that Alex had mapped out exactly what they would be doing. Although Alex had made mistaken assumptions about the market, his style did not allow them to correct him. The people seconded from Finance and Operations had similar experiences.

So it was with a feeling of impending doom that the team left its first full meeting. Reminding everyone of the urgency of completing the programme before peak summer demand, Alex had not asked for any of their expert input, and had allocated all their tasks in extreme detail for the next two months. They were right to be worried. In the following weeks, Alex was in 'tell' mode most of the time. And with little team discussion, people found themselves duplicating each other's work, flying off at tangents, and generally becoming demotivated.

The phone on Alex's desk rang from somewhere beneath the piles of papers which had clearly cost the lives of several Amazonian rain forests. 'Hello, Alex, it's Bob here – could you drop by for a minute? … Yes, now.' Bob looked up from his desk as Alex walked in. 'Alex, I've got some good news, and some bad news – which would you like first?'

Alex elected for the good news first, which was that the Acquisition Review Committee had been reasonably pleased with the progress of Alex's team so far. 'However,' continued Bob, 'we're all worried about whether the rest of the work on this project will get done. You used to be regarded as a good coach and manager – that's why we appointed you to this role – but you seem to have slipped into a mode of real micro-management over the last month. Several of your team members have even asked to be moved off your team. If you're going to turn into a people eater there's no way you will be able to continue managing *this* project. What's gone wrong?'

'There's just not enough time to coach people on this project,' shrugged Alex, who went on to explain all the problems which needed to be addressed. 'In addition,' he continued, 'with only three more months for this project to run, I really don't think that any time I invest in coaching now will generate a major benefit.'

Bob disagreed. 'You have hit a coaching block, Alex. You'll have to overcome it – and fast.' Bob went on to explore in more detail Alex's reluctance to coach. He pointed out that the most common block is where the manager says, 'There just isn't enough time to coach or provide feedback'. However, he pointed out, this is normally an excuse for 'I need to be in complete control – I cannot risk delegating'. Clearly, there are times when this response may be appropriate. But too often these situations are exactly the ones in which the manager needs to do everything possible to unleash the full power of the people with whom s/he is working.

'Well, how do I get around this block?' asked Alex.

'You're good at planning – so why not use your planning skills to plan some *coaching*?' Bob replied, handing Alex a brief note [reproduced on the next two pages]. 'I really want you to work on your people skills, Alex. You're strong in all other dimensions of management, but this could really hold you back.'

Deep down, Alex knew he'd have to do some serious self examination – other aspects of his life were not going well. For example, over the preceding few months, his relationship with his girlfriend Rachel had become very strained. She had accused him of never listening to her, and of always trying to organise everything. He had even insisted on telling her exactly what birthday present she should give her mother. The end had come last week when she had eventually left him. Perhaps he had become a 'control freak' after all.

Late that night he called Sarah for advice. She was on temporary assignment in Hong Kong, and the difference between time zones meant that she would now be at the office.

Working around coaching blocks

Sometimes we do not take up opportunities to coach other people, even though we are well intentioned. Why is this, and what can we do about it?

A major organisation recently conducted research in this area. It compared the coaching behaviour of 80 managers against their in depth psychological profiles. This identified: *(1)* four rationales that the managers typically used, to 'allow' themselves not to coach; *(2)* the real underlying reasons for not coaching in those situations; and *(3)* how they could overcome these blocks (see the chart opposite).

For example, those managers who claimed they did not have enough time to coach were typically people with an unusually high need to control their environment and the people around them.

While the origins of this trait were buried somewhere in the managers' psychology, the exact cause was irrelevant. The important observation was that, for those managers, the best route into coaching was to 'control' how and when they would provide coaching and feedback.

There were three other frequently encountered coaching 'blocks', each with its own likely remedy, as shown on the opposite page.

Coaching blocks and ways around them

Typical 'rationale' for not coaching	Possible 'real' reason	Possible entry into coaching
1 'Not enough time to coach'	I need to be in complete control	Agree very specifically when and how coaching will happen
2 'Coachee won't respond, anyway'	I'm frightened I can't do it	Ask coachee how s/he would like to receive feedback/ coaching
3 'The task won't suffer if I don't coach'	If I ignore it, the problem will go away	Reassess your ability to become a true leader
4 'I might hurt them'	They won't like me	Start where it is safe – someone with whom you get on well, or someone who is good, but could be great

Exercise

Think back to the last time you should have coached or given feedback. Why didn't you? What would have made it easier for you?

Ug's inability to distinguish giving advice from delivering criticism holds up the project at an important stage …

'Instant payoff' coaching can work, though only if delivered well

9

Coaching in a hurry

*In which Alex is still out of control, and benefits
from a dose of instant payoff coaching*

Following his discussion with Bob, Alex had set himself
the aspiration of overcoming his coaching block, and so
unleashing the team's full potential. He was determined not to be a
'control freak' from now on.

Nevertheless, he did know more about the ice cream industry
than anyone else in the company so, very soon, the temptation
to move back into tell mode was too strong. Six weeks later, Alex
still found himself suffering from his inability to let go of any part
of Project Genesis. Things came to a head halfway through the
gruelling schedule which Alex had set for integrating the European
manufacturing operations of the newly created ice cream empire.

Most of the joint manufacturing operations were in France, and
Alex had thought that Tom (who had continued to work with Alex
on Project Genesis, after the original Project Quest) could carry out
the interviews there. Alex would go along to the first few interviews,
then Tom could carry on by himself, while Alex spent more time on
the marketing strategy.

But unfortunately, Alex had early on come to the conclusion
that Tom could not do the interviews by himself. Rather than cancel
the planned meetings, Alex had handled them all himself, writing
up the meeting notes late into the night, then spending an hour or
two on the marketing strategy.

One particular night, he had a bad dream: he was doomed to be
on a very long project which involved interviewing everyone in the
phone book whose telephone number was a prime number. It took
a whole year to do this, by which time a new phone book had been
published …

Alex was working too hard, and he knew it. He went to see Bob, his boss. 'We've got a real problem on the European integration, Bob. We need to renegotiate the timetable.'

Bob saw that it would be impossible to change the timetable: everything had to be ready for the peak sales of ice cream next summer. He also did not want to volunteer more of his own time to the project, because of his other commitments. He had to help Alex build his confidence that there were other ways forward, but he was due to get in a cab to the airport in ten minutes.

'What's the problem?' he asked, remembering the instant payoff coaching technique that he had recently picked up from the new company wide coaching programme.

'Well,' Alex began, 'Tom really isn't skilled at interviewing, and I'm nervous about how the guys in France will react to him. I can't see how I can help him, as well as manage the overall project, as well as complete my own work on the marketing strategy … it's simply too much. Given how much this project is worth to the company, surely we can get agreement to adding another team member – just for a month or two?'

Bob paused before responding. He thought that there may be a better solution – one which would encourage Alex to be less of a 'control freak'. 'Let's explore the issue more fully, Alex. Tell me what you would see if the problem was fixed; don't tell me how we could do it, just tell me what success would look like.'

Alex reflected for a moment. 'Well, Tom would have completed all the interviews, would have built relationships with the key executives in France, and would have drafted a report summarising his findings, which I could discuss with him a few days before the next steering group meeting …'

Alex looked visibly relieved with the semblance of focus he had just created from the chaos, but then panicked, 'But he isn't good enough, he …'

Bob stopped him. 'Before we examine Tom's abilities, tell me the obstacles between where we are now and where you said you'd like us to be.'

As Alex spoke, Bob simply listed the points on a flipchart. He didn't comment on the obstacles, but just asked Alex to look at the completed list, and to indicate where each obstacle lay – in himself, in someone else, or in the situation.

Alex was surprised to see how many of the obstacles were in fact to do with himself, and that relatively few were to do with Tom's abilities. Bob didn't need to ask Alex what he was going to focus on as a next step; Alex volunteered. 'This is great. I can see a way through this without more people, if you would talk to the Chief Executive of the French subsidiary about his people's dismissive attitudes to Tom. We'll send Tom on a one day interviewing course, and I'll see whether I can come off the recruiting taskforce for just a couple of days.' As they ended their ten minute session, Bob went off to the airport and Alex set off down the hall to find Tom.

In the following weeks, Alex tried practising the instant payoff coaching technique and even explained it to Tom in case it helped in France...

Instant payoff coaching

Sometimes you do not have the time or knowledge to complete a full coaching discussion and really build someone's skills, but you do want to help someone who is 'stuck' to complete the task in question.

Using the model shown opposite, you can achieve this in as little as five minutes by helping your coachees to see that they themselves have some responsibility for the situation and that there is something they can do, however small.

Instant payoff coaching

1   Ask the coachee to describe the current issue or problem, with specific examples and a small amount of relevant background.

2   Ask her/him to describe the outcome – paint as specific a 'picture' as possible of how things would be if s/he had sorted out the problem. Do not try to solve the problem, but note down any emerging ideas.

3   With the coachee, list all the obstacles/blocks that lie between 1 and 2. Sort them into three groups:

- Blocks that exist in the coachee (lack of skill/knowledge, low motivation, attitude, etc.)
- Blocks that exist in others (anxious customer, manager stressed and panicking, etc.)
- Blocks in the situation (inadequate resources, shift in deadlines, etc.).

4   Jointly brainstorm ways around these blocks, and possible next steps. Agree an approach, actions and timing.

Exercise

Try this on yourself. If it works, try it with the next person who asks for your advice.

*Frankenstein makes a fundamental error in his 'Jump for Joy'
programme.*

Diagnose your coachee's will, not just skill

10

Taking account of others'
skill and will

In which Alex learns about the Skill/Will matrix

'**A**bout time too,' thought Alex, as Bob gave him the official news of his promotion to senior manager.

'Of course,' added Bob, reading Alex's mind, 'you would have been promoted earlier – based on the project management skills you displayed by completing Project Genesis on time. But we had to be sure that you had the *people* skills too. We had to be sure that you didn't stumble over your coaching blocks. After all, inventories can be managed, but people need to be led.'

Now, three years into his career with the company, Alex had five or six major initiatives to look after. He knew that in his new role he would have to be careful about how he allocated his time – there really was no way in which he could micro-manage all these initiatives at the same time. Fortunately, having glimpsed the power of effective coaching, he had read up more fully on the subject. This was the perfect opportunity to apply the Skill/Will matrix, and he reread the paragraphs from his coaching book.

In some ways, the idea of the Skill/Will matrix is simple, but it needs practice to apply it effectively. The overall concept is that you tailor your style of coaching and management to both the skill and the will of the person you are managing, bearing in mind the task they are trying to accomplish.

For example, if someone really is able to accomplish a given task, and they are motivated to complete it (i.e., high skill and high will), then the appropriate management style would be to Delegate.

However, if the person had low skill and low will – for the task in question – then you would need to be more Directive, at least initially.

For high skill, low will – or vice versa – the manager should use Excite or Guide styles respectively.*

While this sounds simple in theory, there are three main challenges. First, you have to really diagnose the coachee's skill and will, without leaping to conclusions based on prejudice or accepting the coachee's frequent pretence to be 'high skill and high will' at everything. Second, you need to modify dynamically your management or coaching style, as the coachee builds both skill and will. And thirdly, you and your coachee need to share the same diagnosis of the situation and the coachee's skill and will.

Alex thought about Tom, who had now been with the company for about a year. Tom was in charge of the project to identify the company's next acquisition in the frozen food market. Alex knew that Tom was high on will: he was very keen on this role, having dropped enough hints to Alex that he wanted the assignment.

But Alex wasn't so sure about Tom's skill. Tom certainly had the creativity and flexibility which the new project might require. But Alex thought Tom was less strong in strategy and valuation analysis.

Rather than leaping to conclusions, however, Alex decided to have a frank discussion with Tom. He was careful to use genuinely open questions – as opposed to leading ones, and to avoid an accusing tone of voice. This discussion confirmed Alex's initial thoughts, although he was relieved to discover that Tom had carried out several company valuations while with his previous employer.

'High will, fairly high skill' thought Alex. 'I can afford to Delegate and be fairly hands off; but I had better make sure I provide a bit of Guidance in the area of strategy.'

Alex went through a similar process with the four other people who reported directly to him … one more Guide, two Delegates and a Direct. Initially he used an informal, round-about, mode of

* See Appendix 4 (page 126) for descriptions of these styles

discussion – but soon he was comfortable enough with the process to just meet with his people and talk frankly and explicitly about skill and will. He started to feel relieved that he had things in better perspective, and that he could now prioritise his time for the next month or so. Thereafter he'd review progress to see whether he could use more of the Delegate style, to free up further time for himself.

Selecting an appropriate coaching style

The Skill/Will matrix

All too often, we assign a task to someone and the job does not quite get done well enough. Why is this?

One of the most likely reasons is that we have delegated the task to someone who is unwilling – or unable – to complete the job, and have then remained relatively 'hands off' or uninvolved. Alternatively, we may have been too 'hands-on' or directive with a capable person who was quite able to complete the assignment with little assistance from us; we just ended up demotivating her/him.

So whether you are 'coaching' or just 'managing', it is critical to match your style of interaction with the coachee's readiness for the task.

To help you do this, use the Skill/Will matrix:

- First, diagnose the coachee's skill and will to accomplish the task, as indicated on the opposite page

- Then use the matrix to identify the appropriate style of interaction – e.g., you would want to use 'Delegate' if your coachee was high in both skill and will

- Finally, agree with your coachee your diagnosis, and the style you will be using

A few observations:

- Ensure you are addressing the coachee's skill and will to execute the specific task in question – e.g., 'making presentations to the Board of Directors' rather than 'public speaking'

- If you are working with someone over a longer period, you will want them to increase in both will and skill. If they are successful in doing this, you will need gradually to adopt the appropriate styles en route to 'Delegate'

Using the Skill/Will matrix

1   Diagnose whether the coachee's skill and will are high or low, for the specific task to be accomplished:
   ● **Skill** depends on experience, training, understanding, role perception
   ● **Will** depends on desire to achieve, incentives, security, confidence

Skill/Will Matrix

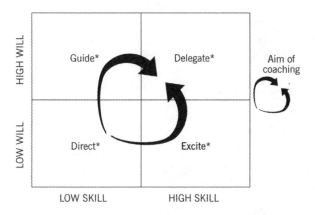

*See Appendix 4 (page 126) for details of each approach

2   Identify the appropriate coaching/management style – e.g., use 'Guide' if the coachee has high will but low skill for the task:

3   Agree your intended approach with your coachee.

Exercise

Recall a time when you were poorly coached or managed. Was your manager's style consistent with your skill and will? Reflect on your current approach to managing someone else. Do steps 1–3 above suggest any changes?

*Doc Gilby, the Dentist, gained trust and built confidence
through his use of Fluffywuffy the hand puppet ... of course
if that didn't work there was always Mr Slap Hammer ...*

Build genuine trust with the 'reluctant' coachee

11 Overcoming a reluctance to being coached

In which Alex learns to overcome the reluctance of one of his coachees

Alex was muttering to himself as he walked down the corridor. Just when he had really begun to master some of the more advanced aspects of coaching, such as the Skill/Will matrix, he had had to endure yet another frustrating and unproductive discussion with Angus, the analyst who was working for Tom on the latest acquisition.

Despite the overwhelming temptation to blame Angus, Alex decided to be more constructive. Applying some self coaching, he tried the GROW model (refer back to Chapter 6) on himself. 'What is my Goal here ... to decide on one thing which might unblock my communications with Angus, so I can deliver some vital feedback. What about the current Reality, then ...' Alex began to recall his encounter with Angus.

'Angus, how are you doing?' Alex had asked as he had entered Angus's office.

'Fine,' had come the rather clipped response.

'Is there anything you would like my help on, while Tom is away on vacation?' In response to the shaken head, Alex had persevered, 'Are you absolutely sure that everything is under control – everything you had agreed with Tom?'

'Absolutely.'

Tom had warned Alex that Angus tended to overestimate his ability, and that he was reluctant to ask for help. Tom had attributed this to the culture at Angus's previous employer, where survival had depended on a continuous show of strength.

Alex offered Angus a chance. 'You are allowed to ask for help around here, you know.' Angus thanked him for the offer, promised to ask for help if needed, and pressed on with his work. As he reflected on the encounter, Alex was puzzled. Surely people knew that they could be open with him.

He thought back to the times when he had been in Angus's situation. As a more junior person, Alex himself had been reluctant to disclose his own needs in new relationships with bosses and peers. He had felt that his 'admissions' might just be used against him. Alex realised that – in discussions with Angus – he had been relying purely on his reputation as a good coach. Perhaps Angus did not trust him.

'So,' thought Alex continuing his self-coaching, 'if trust is the key, what are my Options? Let's see: *(1)* tell him it's OK, *(2)* ask someone else to tell him that I can be trusted, *(3)* let Tom worry about it …' None of the ideas seemed a likely winner. 'All right,' he mused, 'how do I myself assess whether I can trust someone?'

As he was jotting down his thoughts he suddenly remembered a simple idea that he had once read about. This was that you could look at a relationship in terms of an 'emotional bank account', or how much credit (or debit) of goodwill existed between the two people. With strangers, for example, you might have no store of goodwill, and so it would naturally be difficult to get them to do something for you, since there was no reserve of goodwill upon which to draw.

Alex realised that his 'emotional bank account' with Angus was probably overdrawn. Alex had recently made some last minute requests of the team, which had made for some long hours. He also recalled that Angus's father – who lived three hours' drive away – was extremely unwell, and that the weekend working made visits difficult. He also realised that he didn't know very much about Angus's aspirations for himself. It now seemed obvious to Alex that the problem lay not so much in his lacking skills as a coach, but rather in his lacking any real relationship with Angus. Having reviewed his Options, Alex Wrapped up; he knew what to do next.

He found out more about Angus from reading through his last annual appraisal. He made sure that Angus could get home on the following weekend. And he persuaded Angus to go out for a quick drink with him, during which Alex talked about his own career with the company, how he had found it hard to trust new bosses at first, and how difficult it had been to overcome his doubts. He listened carefully to Angus's description of his previous company, and to his fears and aspirations for the job he was now in.

When Alex felt that the moment was right, he asked Angus how he would like to receive feedback or guidance in the future, should the opportunity arise. He stressed that he meant informal, on the job feedback, not the kind that ends up in personnel files. With a more open, trusting relationship, it was easy for Angus to ask for the support he wanted, and he was even willing to ask for Alex and Tom to monitor more closely tasks which were new to him, or of particularly high risk.

Alex reflected that the foundation of all successful coaching is surely an open, trusting relationship with a healthy reservoir of goodwill on both sides.

Dealing with a reluctance to being coached

You may feel that someone would benefit from your coaching, but that s/he appears reluctant to accept your help.

To make progress, you will need to diagnose why the potential coachee is resisting you. He or she may be reluctant to accept any form of coaching by anyone, or may just be reluctant to have you as a coach at the current time.

To take appropriate initiatives, you will need to delve to at least one further level of diagnosis (see opposite page).

Dealing with reluctance

Coachee's mindset	*Options for the coach*

Intrinsic reluctance to be coached

- Unwillingness to admit scope for improvement (in general or in the specific coaching topic)

  - Diagnose the coachee's barriers
  - Emphasise factual evidence for the need to improve ('push' strategy) or …
  - Break through by asking the coachee to coach you ('pull' strategy)

- Mistrust of the organisation

  - Build the trust

- Temporary lack of available time

  - Agree a later session

Reluctance to be coached by you

- Unhelpful historical relationship with you

  - Attempt to 'bury the hatchet'*

- Major difference between her/his style and yours

  - Discuss explicitly, and accept, the 'style' differences if possible* (see Chapter 7)

- Perceived nature of your role in the organisation as being 'highly evaluative'

  - Be explicit about your role – e.g., whether you determine the coachee's remuneration
  - Stress that the coaching is 'non evaluative'*

*Or suggest an alternative coach if all else fails

Exercise

Identify your most 'reluctant' coachee. Develop a plan using the above pointers.

You can't motivate others if they can't see you

Motivating

*In which Alex finds that he can be a good
motivator after all*

A few weeks later, Alex reflected on his three and a half
years with the company. He was glad he had joined
the firm: he seemed to be well-regarded, had been promoted with
reasonable speed, and he admired the people oriented culture which,
he felt sure, had something to do with the company's performance,
which exceeded the industry's average.

In his senior manager role he had thought a bit about the topic
of motivating others. There didn't seem to be many books on the
subject, so he had gradually pieced together tips from watching
what other particularly good managers did.

As he thought about Mary – who had joined his division 18
months ago, and for whom he was preparing an end of year appraisal
session – he wondered how he could apply the three lessons he
had learnt about motivation. These were: *(1)* help the coachee to
understand consciously her/his current level of motivation; *(2)*
help the coachee to fashion a really convincing vision of how well
s/he could perform; and *(3)* support the coachee in her/his efforts
through praise and coaching.

Alex had spent the first 15 minutes of his meeting with Mary
reviewing her performance so far. It had not been easy, since she had
been 'low skill, low will' on many of her recent assignments. Alex
now decided to switch tack for the last 15 minutes of the meeting.

'Mary, it seems to me that you are caught in a negative cycle.
You start off lacking confidence in your abilities; this then leads
you to make only hesitant attempts at the tasks on which you are
engaged; as a result, you deliver below your real potential; and then

you receive less praise than you would hope for. This in turn just exacerbates your lack of confidence.' Alex sketched out the cycle.*

'You know, Alex,' she responded, 'I think you're right. I'd never thought about it this way before; everything just seemed all tangled up.'

'Let's talk about how you can break out of this cycle into a more positive one. Let's figure out something you'd be really good at... any suggestions?'

They discussed a few options, and discarded some which didn't seem relevant enough to Mary's mainstream work activities. In the end, they decided that Mary was going to become the best person in the entire company at making presentations. Alex thought the objective was stretching, but achievable. Although Mary was a bit shy, she was a key figure in the local amateur dramatic group.

'Now, how are we going to get there?' asked Alex. Mary had perked up as the result of the conversation so far, but now gulped and paled. Alex bit his lip and resisted the temptation to dive in and rescue her. Eventually, Mary came up with a surprisingly rich stream of her own ideas, ranging from making the prize draw at the departmental Christmas party, through to running the induction session for people who were just joining the company.

'And what type of help do you think you need?' probed Alex.

'I think I can handle most of this myself!' responded a re-energised Mary, whose ideas ranged from taking a one day course in presenting herself with more impact, through to noting the presentation techniques of famous people as they appeared on television. 'All I'd ask is that you give me some feedback whenever you see me make a presentation.'

'What on earth have you done to Mary while I've been away?' It was the long lost Sarah standing at Alex's door.

Sarah had just returned from her posting to the company's Hong

*See page 67

Kong operation. She had worked with Mary before. But now, several weeks after the annual appraisal session with Alex, Mary seemed a different person.

It turned out that Mary was getting much better at making presentations. But – perhaps more importantly – her growing self confidence in this area was already spilling over into other areas of her work. She was indeed much more motivated. Alex was beginning to think that the time he had invested during the appraisal session had been well worthwhile, and he was glad that he had not confined himself to merely running through the company's standard appraisal form with Mary.

'Well, how were things in Hong Kong?' enquired Alex. 'I tried to call you several times, but you had always just left for some part of South East Asia.'

'It's a long story,' said Sarah. 'But I really learned a lot about managing in an environment with a completely different culture.'

Motivation

The golden rules of motivation:

1 **Know where your coachees are** in the cycle of motivation or demotivation shown opposite.

2a **Work on their confidence**, if they are in the uppermost cycle, as it's about the only thing you can affect directly. Do this by:

● Working with them to develop a vision of how good they could be at completing a specific task, or playing a specific role

● Recognising that improved performance in an area which might not be critical to their mainstream activities usually has very positive spin-off benefits to their 'core' activities.

2b **Work on praise** if they are in the lower cycle.

3 **Identify their needs for support and/or training**, even if it is to be provided by the coachee themself or by a third party.

4 **Know what most motivates your coachees**. Everyone has different motivating factors (see Appendix 5, page 128).

Cycles

NEGATIVE CYCLE OF DEMOTIVATION

Lack of confidence

Hesitant attempts

Poor results

Unsatisfying feedback

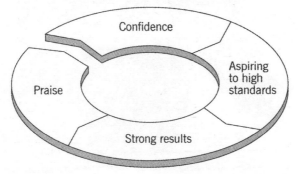

POSITIVE CYCLE OF MOTIVATION

Confidence

Aspiring to high standards

Strong results

Praise

Exercise

- Name four people you work with, identify which cycle they are in and whether you can help them do even better.
- Have your team complete Appendix 5 (page 128), and compare the results, which will differ surprisingly between respondents.

Although Friday afternoon 'Postboy Racing' had been a popular pastime where Lars came from, he still had quite a bit to learn about Frimly and Booth office culture …

Take time to anticipate cultural differences

13 Recognising cultural differences

In which Alex discovers how cultural differences affect coaching

Alex found himself pinned to his seat as flight MA245 took off, ultimate destination Moravia, via Paris. Project Genesis – the integration of Cones and Tubs into the company – was now fully completed, but the company had just made another acquisition to make it the largest ice cream producer in Eastern Europe.

The following morning he found himself in the boardroom of the new Moravian subsidiary, ready for his first full meeting with the local management team. Alex knew the meeting was critical, and knew that it would not be easy to manage this far flung arm of the company from London. So he had to take every opportunity to build the credibility of 'Head Office' as soon as possible.

He had decided to have dinner with the local Strategy Director, Jan, the previous evening to agree how they would run the management meeting. Jan would start off with the agreed presentation on the benefits of the 'merger', then there would be a free format discussion, followed by a tour of the plant. Alex had met with Jan only once before, but had gained the impression that he was very pushy. So Alex had spent a few minutes coaching him on how to 'soften' his style.

Alex cringed as Jan delivered his presentation to the assembled managers. 'Oh no,' thought Alex, 'what a disaster!'

He knew that Moravians typically pulled no punches. They communicated in a very forthright manner. But surely Jan was going too far. What about the coaching session which Alex had had with him the night before?

Why was Jan not using the softer approach which they had

discussed? And what had happened to the comments on which they had agreed as face saving measures for the local Chief Executive?

Alex searched in vain for a way to intercede as Jan increased the tempo. He felt the perspiration on his brow. 'At least,' he thought, 'I know how frank to be in my feedback to Jan as soon as this meeting is over!'

Perhaps it was the pressure, perhaps it was the local Moravian brew he had consumed the night before, perhaps it was the jet lag, but Alex seemed to lose touch with reality for what seemed like only an instant.

The next thing he knew the audience was on its feet – a standing ovation! Jan had wowed the Moravians and won them over.

Later that day, Alex reflected on how he might have managed things differently. Although things had worked out OK in the end, Alex concluded that he'd be more careful next time he coached someone from an obviously different culture. He would think in advance about the most important cultural differences between himself, the coachee, and the coaching context.

Alex realised he should have listened more to Jan over dinner, perhaps discussing openly the cultural issues relating to the forth-coming meeting – rather than presumptuously coaching him on how to soften his style. Nevertheless, if Alex did have to coach Jan again, he would probably be much more frank in his advice, to match Jan's cultural background.

Furthermore, Jan – like Alex – was used to operating in an envi-ronment without much hierarchy. However, if Jan had been used to a more hierarchical environment and had been more deferential to his 'bosses', Alex reflected that he would have had to exercise care that Jan would not interpret a brainstormed idea as a direct order.

Similarly, Alex realised, the meaning – and importance – of 'teamwork' can differ significantly or subtly between cultures, with implications for the senior manager who is attempting to build a team.

Alex boarded the Boeing 727 that would take him home. He was glad that he'd decided to stop over in Paris for the weekend, and was even more delighted to have discovered that Sarah would be there too. He wanted to discuss her experiences in Hong Kong, and compare notes on how to be an effective manager in an unfamiliar culture.

Cultural differences

When coaching someone from a different culture, s/he may well act – or react – differently from what you are used to:

- Cultural differences do not arise only from national, racial or religious origins – e.g., people new to your organisation may still be heavily influenced by the culture of their previous employer
- These differences can result in higher or lower levels of perceived performance, and in more or less need for – and acceptance of – feedback
- When working with multinational teams, or individuals from cultures different from yours, be explicit with yourself, and ideally with them, about the implications of cultural differences
- Above all, commit to building shared expectations – in terms of management style, adherence to deadlines, frequency of progress checks, need for creativity, etc.

For further details, see *Cultures and Organisations* by Geert Hofstede.

Four cultural dimensions

Cultures – both national and organisational – differ along many dimensions. Four of the most important ones are indicated below:

Dimension	Implication for the coach
● **Directness** (get to the point versus imply the messages)	Tailor style of feedback appropriately
● **Hierarchy** (follow orders versus engage in debate)	Position coaching relationship carefully vis-à-vis organisational reporting relationship
● **Consensus** (dissent is accepted versus unanimity is needed)	Select from full repertoire of ask/tell styles – see pages 8 and 9
● **Individualism** (individual winners versus team effectiveness)	Reflect on focus of coaching – e.g. whether or not to focus on teamwork

Exercise

Recall the last time you had difficulty working with someone from another culture. What went wrong? Why? Could you have avoided the problem? Would it have been worth doing?

As Dr Peterson and Professor Forbes slug it out over who has first use of the Nobo board, the rest of the UN Peace Mission start laying odds …

Know how to set up teams well

In which Alex discovers that he has become a recognised team leader

By the time Alex turned up at the party to celebrate Sarah's promotion, the room was already full. Sarah was both highly popular and widely respected as a manager, so attendance was high.

Glass in hand, Alex squeezed away from the crowded bar, and found space within listening distance of a small group of people. One of them, Tom, had recently joined Alex's taskforce which was developing the company's three year plan, and the others seemed to be quizzing him. Alex eavesdropped attentively from his position behind the pot plant.

'What's it like working with this Alex guy?' asked someone. 'I hear he sets a pretty punishing schedule, and I know he used to be a real people eater.'

'I think that's a thing of the past,' replied Tom. 'We just had a kickoff meeting on this planning taskforce of his, and I must say he seems pretty smart and good with people.'

'How do you mean?'

'Well, he had set the meeting up really well. There are five of us on this taskforce, and he'd sent us all a copy of the work plan which he'd drafted, several days in advance.'

'What's the big deal about that?' asked another member of the group.

'The point is, he made it very clear that he'd welcome our comments on the plan,' Tom continued. 'He must have done a bit of research on each of us, too – even the people seconded in from other departments – because he sort of knew which areas each of us could best comment on.

'Anyway, we got together for the meeting, and he gave a really convincing speech about how important the work is – and he really managed to build some team spirit.

'And then he handed out copies of the last annual appraisal which his boss had given him – not just the good bits, but the things at which he's meant to be improving.'

'But why on earth did he do that?' asked someone else.

'Well, he didn't tell us why in so many words, but the effect was quite powerful, because it made people really open up when he asked each of us to explain what we wanted personally to get out of this project. And we really believed him when he said that this was going to be a team in which we gave each other a lot of feedback, and helped each other out if we needed to.

'We even spent five minutes on which parts of the project looked the most busy, to check that the inevitable late hours weren't going to interfere too much with our personal lives.

'Then we talked through our roles and responsibilities. You know, he actually listened to what we had to say, and we rearranged that draft work plan quite a bit. When we left the meeting, we all knew pretty much what we were meant to do, and felt that this was going to be a real team effort. We even agreed to have a team appraisal session* in three weeks' time, to check that our teamwork was up to scratch.'

'You don't need a PhD in rocket science to do that kind of thing,' quipped a more cynical bystander.

'No, you don't,' replied Tom, 'but tell me if you've ever had a team meeting like that. And that thing about sharing his own annual appraisal – the only reason it had impact was that it took some courage on his part.'

*See Appendix 6 (page 130)

Alex could not suppress a self contented smirk as he sidled away to find Sarah. 'So, that was what "corridor talk" sounded like first hand …!' he thought. 'And it's true, you don't necessarily need to be a rocket scientist to be a great team leader.'

He also thought about how valuable his skills in one to one coaching had been when it came to building and managing a team.

Coaching in the team context

Some teams work hard, have fun and get the job done. Other teams are miserable and ineffective, despite the fact that all the team members are working twice as hard as normal. Why is this?

In their book *The Wisdom of Teams*, Jon Katzenbach and Douglas Smith identified the six basic requirements for good teamwork illustrated below. While it is beyond our scope to address each of these basics, let's review the one most related to coaching – the well defined working approach.

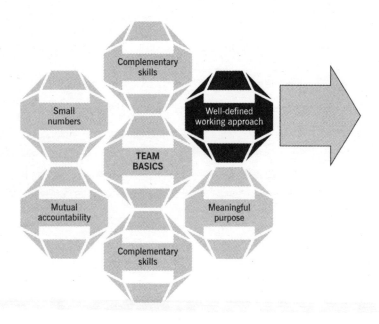

Define your approach

A well defined working approach is integral to effective teamwork and essential for a positive coaching environment.
Constructive characteristics include:

1 The leader holds a half day meeting within the first two weeks, to agree ground rules and 'team charter' – e.g.,
   - Individuals' objectives
   - Working hours and likely 'crunch' periods

2 Individuals discuss personal needs for skills development openly and early
   - Set example by sharing fast personal performance review with team
   - Set clear expectations for feedback

3 The whole team participates in drafting work plan

4 All team members feel comfortable providing and receiving ongoing feedback and 'blowing the whistle' if necessary

5 The team reviews how it is working every six weeks, or more frequently if needed, or after major milestones (e.g., after publishing a report).

Exercise

Consider points 1–5 in the context of your current project and suggest/take corrective action if needed.

Use the power of questions that reframe

15

Using the power of the question

In which Alex again sees that a question can be more powerful than a suggestion

Alex's phone whistled the notification that a text message had arrived. 'U free 4 a drink? Need ur advice! Colin.'

Colin was one of Alex's peers and now ran the company's fast food business in the UK. They had met when working on an acquisition together and had become close friends during the last few years.

The following Saturday they met for a coffee at a convenient Starbucks and Colin explained that he been offered a new role running the company's newly-formed US operations.

'As you know,' said Colin, 'I am having a great time in my current role. I've finally got the business into growth mode, and at last I've established a really strong team. It would seem crazy to leave it just now.'

'So... ?' Alex prompted.

'It's just that I've been with this division for such a long time. Perhaps it's time for a change?'

'Sounds like the current role is pretty good,' replied Alex, stirring the chocolate into the cappuccino. 'Why bother moving? I wouldn't take the risk if I were you.'

Colin looked surprised. 'That's easy for you to say!' he replied, 'you've had a pretty varied career. But I've only ever worked in this one division since joining the one company. I need a change.'

'I see... How about writing down the pros and cons?'

'Thanks for that brilliant insight, Alex. I can assure you that I have looked at all the pros, and all the cons as well.'

'And the risks versus the returns?'

'Yes, those too.'

Alex could feel that he wasn't really helping. 'Hmm ... so how can I help you?' he asked. He hesitated – wondering whether to use the GROW model, or whether that might be overkill. 'Seems like you have all the information you need in order to make the decision. And it sounds like you've analysed it all as far as you can. Have you discussed it with Carol?'

'Of course,' replied Colin, now slightly irate. 'She says she'll be happy with whatever I do.'

Alex, master of strategic thinking, possessor of a fine intellect, and experienced manager could think of no further process that would help.

Colin's predicament was of course an oft-encountered one. He was trying to choose between two options but was impaled on the horns of his dilemma. He had amassed a vast amount of information through interview and research, and had analysed it all conscientiously. But the more he considered the pros and cons, the more his question entangled him. The more he sought to find a new way of thinking about it. The more he was dragged back to the old way of thinking about it. The fact that it was an important decision made it worse, as his anxiety made him particularly alert not to overlook any facet of the issue. He had sought advice from those whom he trusted but still had not found an answer. He needed a completely new way to view the problem.

'OK,' ventured Alex, 'just for a moment, assume you've taken the new role ... Now tell me: why did you take it?'

Colin looked perplexed at first, then started to smile at the unexpected question, 'Alex, you always did have a trick up your sleeve! I haven't thought about it from that angle before.'

'Go on then, tell me why.'

Colin paused for a moment and had a go at articulating his imagined decision. 'Well, I thought about staying in my old role, because the operation was doing well, I had built a great team, it was a short commute from home, and I liked my boss...'

Alex interrupted, 'Sounds like you're about to do pros and cons again, but in disguise! Just tell me why you really took the new role.'

Colin had another go, but could not get excited by his answer which rested merely on the vague notion of 'doing something different.' He soon realised that he did not really want to move his family to the US, and that he would instead use his strong brand within the company to negotiate a transition to a role that had greater variety.

Alex realised how many angles a given issue can be tackled from – and how a simple question can shift the viewpoint to one that shows an answer.

The power of the question

Coaches sometimes offer suggestions to their coachees, and managers often issue instructions. But as we saw in chapter one, that most powerful coaching is non-directive: it is based on asking excellent questions – especially when there is a Gordian Knot of a predicament that cannot be untied, and so must be cut instead.

Those who criticise the non-directive approach may erroneously feel that this approach is too easy, or that the non-directive coach is in some way lazy. Yet the power of the non-directive approach is confirmed by the findings of neuroscience.

- Coaching is usually employed when the coachee would perform better by doing something in a way that differs from the hitherto habitual way, or requires seeing something in a new light.

- Yet, when confronted with a new way of doing something (even if from a suggestion that is believed to be well-intentioned), the brain reacts adversely. Specifically, a region called the anterior cingulate cortex starts to register a conflict versus the brain's existing schemas, and the amygdala sounds an alarm to resist.

- By asking an excellent question, the coachee's alarm system is to some extent bypassed and his or her brain becomes engaged in a process of exploration rather than of defence.

The page opposite offers the coach a selection of ways in which to help the coachee explore issues from new and productive angles. For an extreme and valuable version of non-directive questioning, see *Clean Language* by Wendy Sullivan and Judy Rees.

Asking questions that reframe from a new perspective

Perspective: from ...	Example coaching question
Afar	Is this the right issue to be addressing?
Above (Super-Ego)	How would you explain this to a person strongly affected by your decision?
Left (logic)	What does your head tell you?
Right (emotion)	What does your heart tell you?
Behind (the past)	Which route is most consistent with your life/values/success formula so far?
In front (the future)	How does this fit with your picture of where you want to be?
Below (fears)	Are you operating out of fear; is this good?
(Imagined) retrospect	Imagine you have already chosen the course of action – now tell me why you chose it?
Someone else's point of view	How would he/she/your ally/your enemy/your father/your mother etc react? [or want you to react?]

Exercise

For the next issue that you or a coachee encounters, ask a question that attempts to reframe the issue from a productive new angle.

Armed to the teeth with his sixth sense and no torch,
Ted presses on.

Coaches work with observable facts,
not just 'gut feel'

16

Coaching caveats

In which Alex goes too far with pop psychology

Alex had just been on a long vacation, to celebrate his fourth anniversary with the company. He had returned with a tan and a general feeling of well being – particularly since his relationship with his new girlfriend had endured its first holiday test.

He ploughed through his in tray with the help of his assistant, and as she was leaving he asked her for an update on the rumour, scandal and gossip from the office grapevine.

'Not much to report,' she began, 'It's been pretty quiet. All I've really heard is that Tim and Mary have had a bit of a bust up.'

Mary was one of Alex's most able managers. She was spending a lot of time with Tim, from the marketing department, on a taskforce to revamp the company's research and development process. Although progress had been excellent, Alex had noticed that there had been friction between the two of them.

'Time for a coaching session,' thought Alex, recalling the GROW framework which he had used so successfully over the years.

He met with Mary and they agreed that teamwork would be a good topic to discuss.

'How are you getting on with Tim?' asked Alex.

'Not too well,' responded Mary, 'we just don't seem to be on the same wavelength.'

Mary thought for a moment. 'Actually, we get on OK when there are just two of us. The friction seems to arise when there are other people in the room.'

Alex was sure he knew what was happening. He'd noticed that Mary had been very competitive in the company's recent annual softball tournament. Mary's problems with Tim conveniently confirmed Alex's hypothesis that she felt a need to assert herself when the audience grew larger than one.

'Do you sometimes feel a need to prove yourself in meetings with Tim?' he asked.

Mary pondered.

'... and particularly when there are other people present?' Alex continued. He knew he was taking a chance, but he had a strong hunch that he was on the right track.

'Well, er ... no, not really,' said Mary.

'And are you perhaps more competitive with men than with women?'

'I don't think so,' said Mary, starting to get defensive now.

'Sometimes these things go back to childhood,' continued Alex. 'Perhaps you felt competitive towards your brother when you were younger?'

Now Mary was really beginning to wonder what was happening. She glanced nervously around the room, noticing as she did so several well-thumbed books by Freud lying on the bookshelf.

'Actually,' Mary replied politely, 'I've always got on very well with my family.'

Alex pursued the point for a few more minutes until a call from abroad interrupted their meeting. It was Mary's chance to escape from the amateur psychologist's couch, and she took it.

Within a few days, Mary had resolved her problem with Tim. When Alex noticed the change he had a chat with Mary, and was surprised to find that their problems had arisen purely from a few specific misunderstandings. Then he thought back to his ineffective coaching session, and realised that he had probably been barking up the wrong tree.

Perhaps it was a bad idea to do too much psychologising in a coaching session.. 'A little learning is a dangerous thing ...' he recalled. Next time he would listen more, and focus on the facts of the situation, taking them more at face value.

However, Alex had another problem which he was to discover

the next day, and which would take several months of hard effort to sort out. In the period prior to his vacation he had spent so much time on coaching, motivating and feeding back to people that he had taken his eye off the underlying business issues. Some tough decisions had been called for. But, rather than take those decisions himself, he had delegated them to his teams. 'After all,' he had thought, 'my teams are *empowered*.' But unfortunately he had over-delegated the process of resolving several important strategic issues.

Coaching caveats

When helping to build skills, great coaches – while aware of the principles of psychology – often work in a more straightforward manner with observed behaviours and actions.

By way of analogy, we know how to switch channels on a TV set without knowing the details of the circuits inside. Consequently, bear in mind the overall guidelines for coaching indicated on the opposite page.

Furthermore, the skilled business manager – unlike the 'empowerment gone mad' coach – knows where to inject a dose of firm decision making.

Coaching caveats

1 **Don't become too psychological:**

Do	Don't
Focus on helping the coachee with specific tasks	Search for psychological problems which 'might' exist
Be business-like and frank	Try to be 'nice'
Check you are addressing a real issue	Miss the point
Moderate the amount and depth of your coaching	Overcoach
Refer people with major personal problems to a qualified counsellor	Bite off more than you can chew

2 **Don't lose sight of strategic and operational issues which need your decisive action**

'I'm glad we had this little chat, Eddie, it turns out you're not the sneaky, snivelling, crying-in-the-washroom type I'd mistaken you for – when you get back to your office order yourself a new swivel chair, like mine ...'

Providing 'upward' feedback to the boss can have its benefits

17

Giving feedback upwards

In which Alex discovers that it's easy to provide upward feedback, and that it can be rewarding

Alex had eventually resolved the strategic issues which he had let slip several months earlier. But, with only six weeks to go until the shareholders' Annual General Meeting, he was growing nervous.

He was supposed to be helping Peter, the Chairman, with his speech but whenever they met they always seemed to end up wasting a lot of time. First, Peter was rather disorganised and took ages to retrieve relevant papers from accidental hiding places. Second, people who happened to be passing Peter's office tended to just drop by and interrupt their meetings.

'Boy,' thought Alex as the fourth person in as many minutes knocked on the door, 'Peter could really use some feedback and coaching on time management and personal organisation. I wonder if anyone has ever mentioned it to him in the past.'

As their meeting eventually drew to a close, Alex moved towards the door, plucked up courage, and turned to Peter. 'By the way, the company wide coaching programme that we launched several years ago seems to be going really well. In fact, I've found the upward feedback from it has been very helpful – not just soft stuff: the suggestions have really helpded me work smarter. How have you found it?'

'I must admit I haven't really had time to ask for any feedback, although I know the programme is meant to be for everyone.'

Alex paused in case Peter felt like inviting some feedback, but of course he waited in vain. He took a slightly deeper breath than normal and feigned nonchalance. 'Of course, we could just take a few minutes at the end of our next meeting if you'd like any suggestions from me,' he volunteered. The Chairman was apparently receptive, and Alex made a mental note to gather his thoughts prior to next week's rendezvous.

As that next meeting ended, Alex girded his loins. 'Well,' he began, 'how about that upward feedback?'

'I'm not sure I've got time for a discussion now,' replied Peter.

'But perhaps there are ways for you to actually create more time for yourself,' continued Alex undaunted. 'I've been giving it some thought.' The Chairman looked up, surprised but intrigued.

Alex said that he had a few ideas which might be helpful, but decided (remembering to use his full repertoire of ask/tell styles) to ask Peter what he thought would be the most useful area to cover. Peter was definitely interested in the topic of time management.

Alex suggested that they focus on the 45 minute meeting which they had just concluded, to see whether there were any clues to greater effectiveness.

After some discussion, Peter volunteered that he really should have his assistant set up a better filing system; that way he wouldn't spend ages looking for lost papers. They also brainstormed a further 20 ideas, all of which had some merit.

Just when Peter thought they had finished the discussion, Alex decided to broach what he was afraid would be the most sensitive area. He knew that Peter liked to maintain a strict 'open door policy', but Alex was sure that the frequent interruptions which had frustrated him during the last three quarters of an hour probably continued all day.

'A further thought, Peter; how about asking your assistant to screen out more of the people who drop by on a casual basis? I'm sure that would save you a lot of time, by allowing you to concentrate on one thing at a time. For example, we must have had 15 interruptions in the last 45 minutes. I know you like to have an open door policy, but there is a difference between the door being ajar and it being agape!'

'Well, Alex, I always like people to feel they can contact me whenever they need to.'

'Yes,' responded Alex, 'but the result is that everyone who has ever had a meeting with you (and therefore been interrupted by others) feels entirely at home "getting their own back" and making up for the time they lost in their original meeting with you, through interrupting the next person you are seeing.' Alex realised he was going all out, and wondered how Peter would respond.

Peter was genuinely surprised – he had no idea of the dynamic which his open door policy had set up. However, he balked at the prospect of forgoing his previously enshrined principle.

Having gone this far, Alex was not about to give up. 'Why don't you try an experiment for one week, Peter. After all, what's the worst that could happen?'

Peter did try it for a week. It worked, and he suddenly found himself with much more time than he'd ever had.

He went to find Alex. 'I just wanted to thank you for the "upward" feedback. That open door policy worked when I started the company 30 years ago, but not now that we're a large multinational. You were right about that open door policy. Actually, I've revamped a few other working habits too.'

'Good chap, that Alex,' muttered the Chairman to himself as he headed off down the corridor.

Establishing an effective environment for upward feedback

Giving upward feedback is the same as giving feedback downwards, or 'sideways' to peers, provided you establish an explicit contract with your 'boss' to do so.

- Most people really appreciate constructive, timely, actionable and sensitively delivered feedback.
- However, you may sometimes feel that it is more difficult to deliver than it really is.
- Creating an environment and relationship which supports mutual giving and receiving of feedback is best done at the beginning of a task or working relationship, before there is any actual feedback to be given.

Upward feedback tips

Useful ways to position the offer

- 'Would you like to receive feedback? If so, about what in particular, and in what form?'
- 'If I have any observations which might be helpful to you or your team, how would you like me to communicate them?'
- 'Is there any specific part of our work together where feedback from me would be particularly helpful?'
- 'It feels nerve-wracking to give feedback to you because you are so busy/tired/preoccupied/focused. How can I best get through to you in these situations?'

Suggestions for delivering the feedback

- The first few times, just deliver positive messages that affirm or reinforce. This will allow you to get into the right habits and protocols.
- Then move on to feedback that may require your boss to change. Make the logic and potential impact clear, eg: 'The team is floundering ... they want more direction ... perhaps you could lead some weekly communications sessions ...'

Exercise

At the beginning of your next piece of work, agree with your 'boss' how you will handle upward feedback.

Become eloquent in the language of setting goals

18

Becoming eloquent in the language of setting goals

In which Alex stumbles across more advanced techniques for setting goals

ate one evening, Alex was Googling dextrously to find some creative ideas he could slip into the speech he was drafting for the Chairman. But he was having difficulty concentrating – he kept thinking about his poor old uncle who had just had a knee replaced. Alex knew the rehabilitation could be both painful and lengthy.

He decided to see whether the internet had any advice, and as usual landed on a page with unexpected content. The site did mention rehabilitation and recovery after knee operations, but was in the form of a reference to a psychology experiment quoted in a book called *The Power of Habit* by Charles Duhigg. Alex became absorbed by the material, and because it also related to an issue he was dealing with at work on goal-setting, he exceeded his self-imposed five minutes of reading about it.

The psychology paper provided evidence that written goals are much more powerful than unwritten ones. Perhaps that was to be expected; but what surprised Alex was the magnitude of the difference. Patients who had written down their goals had started walking in almost half the time required by patients who had not. They had started getting in and out of their chairs, unassisted, in almost a third of the time. They were putting on their shoes, and making themselves meals far sooner than patients who had not written down their goals.

Alex perused on, interested since he was about to refresh his process for setting and reviewing his team's annual performance. It appears that people who write down their goals almost invariably are drawn into a degree of basic planning in order to decide what goal to actually set, and it is clear that they are already starting to envision how they could break down overall goals into manageable components. It reminded Alex of Churchill's maxim that 'plans are irrelevant; planning is everything.' The true value of goal-setting and planning is to breathe life into the process of achievement. But it does not work nearly so well if you don't commit to uttering the plan into the record!

Alex also recalled something he had read in a book called *Hope* by Charles Snyder. Snyder, the world expert on researching hope, believed that a) hopefulness leads to stronger performance in tasks, including swifter recovery from medical conditions; and b) that hope is built from three components: having a clear and valued goal, having 'waypower' (the ability to see many different pathways to achieving that goal), and having 'willpower' (the agency or energy to pursue the pathways). By writing down goals, we start to anticipate how we will achieve those goals, and start to build our waypower. Our brains just do not have enough working memory to do all that without committing the goals to paper.

It was getting late, but Alex followed a few more internet links in the rich seam on goal-setting that he had struck...

Several websites by sports coaches made it clear that sportspeople have thought deeply about how to set goals for individuals and for teams. One important distinction they make is between three types of goal: process goals ("hit a harder serve"), performance goals ("serve more aces"), and outcome goals ("win Wimbledon"). Alex reflected that shareholders in the modern corporate world are far more interested in outcomes or so-called output measures, than they are in process improvement or so-called input measures. Yet many top athletes and their coaches believe that process goals are far more valuable since you can practise reaching a process goal (and get feedback on it) everyday – not just once a year when Wimbledon comes along. You are far more likely to set a goal that is demanding if it is a process goal because, if you fail to meet it, your failure will not be so public as failing to achieve a demanding outcome goal.

○◯○

Before returning to the Chairman's speech, Alex jotted down a few notes on goal setting, indicated on the following page, and mapped out how he would apply them in his role as coach, team leader, and, increasingly, as a senior manager in the company.

Better goal-setting

The first step in the GROW model (Chapter 6) provides the opportunity for the coach to explore and clarify a subset of the coachee's goals: those goals that he or she wants to be coached on.

However, a broader perspective is sometimes required on how to set effective goals – for example when the coach is also the manager or team leader, or when a mentoring relationship may benefit from a more holistic examination of the mentee's objectives.

● The oft-quoted, memorable, but somewhat superficial framework for setting goals is SMART: aim to set goals that are Specific, Measureable, Action-oriented, Realistic, and Timely (you'll find this mnemonic in slightly varying forms).

● More recent research suggests the importance to the coach and coachee (and manager / team member) of several considerations that are more fundamental, as indicated on the facing page.

● The expert coach is also aware of how goal-setting links to related subjects such as Hope, Trust, and Motivation.

Checklist for setting better goals

- Have you used **process** goals, **performance** goals, and **outcome** goals in the correct balance, as described earlier in this chapter?

- Are the goals **challenging enough**? Provided the performer is self-efficacious (confident) and has access to the relevant skills, more challenging goals will result in stronger performance.

- Is the performer **committed** to the goals? Experiments in social psychology suggest that people become committed if they have taken steps in the required direction that are voluntary, visible, irrevocable, and specific. For example the performer has, of his own free will, made a public declaration of the precise goals he is aiming for.

- Have the goals been **written down**? Written goals can be approximately twice as effective as unrecorded ones.

- Are the goals **SMART** (Specific, Measureable, Action-oriented, Realistic, and Timely)?

- Have you given **early and continuing feedback** regarding performance versus the goals?

- As the leader, are you using the '**High Performance Cycle**' to maximum effect? This is the process of setting goals dynamically, to reflect continual increases in team members' satisfaction, commitment, and ability?

Exercise

Check your own goals (or those of someone you are coaching or who reports to you) against the above list.

Mentor someone, and be mentored

19 Mentoring

In which Alex discovers that he is a mentor

With the Annual General Meeting out of the way, Alex had – in addition to his many other roles within the company – resumed his involvement in recruiting. He and several colleagues were discussing a candidate and it was time for the vote. All those who believed that the company should offer Donald the job were to raise their hands. Alex's hand went up, along with everyone else's.

He felt that Donald would be a great addition to the company. Alex thought that he had a few rough edges, but that these could be smoothed off fairly easily. Like Alex five years earlier, Donald's first position would be in strategic planning.

A month later, Alex found himself to be Donald's official mentor, in the new company wide mentoring programme. As no one really knew what a mentor was meant to do, beyond taking the 'mentee' out for a quick welcoming lunch, Alex decided to go back to first principles in his search for an answer. A quick Google came up with:

> *Mentor. A guide, a wise friend and counsellor. In Homer's* Odyssey, *Mentor was an old friend of Odysseus to whom the latter entrusted his home and his son Telemachus. The goddess Minerva assumed the form of Mentor to help Telemachus in his search for Odysseus who had left Ithaca for Troy.*

'Well what on earth does one do to become a guide, a wise and faithful counsellor,' he thought, 'short of becoming a classical deity?'

Over the next few months, Alex discovered that being a mentor was a lot like being a coach. First, there were times when the mentor could help the mentee to raise her/his spirits – and aspirations. Sometimes this involved using the skills of motivation that Alex had picked up earlier in his career; at other times Alex merely had a discussion that helped Donald to stand back from the problems of the moment, and to see his work and life in a broader context.

Then there were the times when Alex just provided a listening ear. He knew that Donald did not necessarily want Alex to help him with a specific problem, nor to log a concern 'officially'. Donald merely wanted to get something off his chest, and to know that someone senior cared enough to listen.

Sometimes Alex did need to shift into a more hands-on role, helping Donald to think through his options. These discussions normally focused on broader career issues, rather than the more task specific issues addressed by a coach.

On other occasions, Alex provided information which Donald might not easily have gained from other sources – such as when he explained the company's emerging strategy in East Asia, and how Donald might use his knowledge of Mandarin to further his career.

Finally, there were times when Alex was the only person who would take on the task of advising Donald on a few changes in style which 'might not go amiss'. Like the time when Donald had started to wear green suits with pink shirts and brown shoes: it wasn't against company policy, but it didn't exactly enhance his credibility. And no one else had felt like giving the feedback.

Alex had also learned to avoid playing certain roles which, at first glance, might appear to be part of a mentor's job description. For example, he had become very careful not to wade in with lots of advice. There were times when he was too far removed from the specific facts of a complicated situation to know what the correct answer was. It was then that he focused on helping Donald to come up with his own answers – just as the effective parent helps the child to become a problem solver rather than a follower of 'orders-dressed-up-as-advice'.

Alex also tried to avoid being a 'rescuer'. He knew that it would not help Donald in the long run if he 'took over' any of Donald's problems. For example, Donald was having issues with his boss, who was a close friend of Alex's. It would have been easy for Alex to have a quiet word with his friend, but he resisted the temptation. He knew that Donald would learn more from figuring out and implementing the answer for himself. Donald would also have more confidence to solve a similar problem next time without having to turn to Alex.

Later, Alex reflected on the time he had spent mentoring Donald. He hadn't spent too many hours on it, but there were certainly other things for which he could have used the time. He concluded that there were some intangible benefits to being a mentor, such as those which Sarah had described in her article in the company magazine several years ago, but that was about it.

Just as Alex was turning his attention to other matters, Donald turned up. 'Alex, I've never really thanked you for all your advice. I just want you to know that you have had a real impact on me. You have even helped me indirectly with my relationship with my girl-friend. I'm not sure if you know, but she's the Chairman's daughter, and we're going to get married. I've already told my future father-in-law what a great guy you are.'

'Well,' thought Alex, 'perhaps there is such a thing as divine justice, after all.'

Some weeks later, Alex was clearing his desk as he prepared to go on holiday. He swiped his phone and right-clicked the voice-recording app to update it in case he had any unusual ideas while on vacation. He had completed all his preparations for the meeting that the Board would have while he was away..

And on his way home he picked up the airline tickets that would take him to Greece …

Mentoring

Mentoring and coaching are very similar activities. The only real difference is that the coach focuses on building the coachee's ability to accomplish **specific tasks**, whereas the mentor has a wider perspective. The mentor typically has a **longer term relationship** with the mentee, or is a counsellor on a **broader range of issues** at any given time.

There are a number of different mentoring roles you could find yourself playing – as an 'official' mentor if your organisation has a system for helping recently hired people, or as a longer term, friendship based mentor who counsels someone for a significant part of his or her career. Between these two extremes lie a variety of other types of relationship.

However, all mentoring roles use all or most of the seven types of assistance indicated opposite.

Seven types of mentoring assistance

Type of assistance	How to do it
1 Helping the mentee to a positive mental attitude	See *Motivation*, pages 66 and 67
2 Listening when the mentee has a problem; identifying the mentee's feelings and legitimising them	Provide a 'listening ear', without a judgemental response. Explore options if appropriate
3 Providing appropriate information when needed	See *Providing Feedback*, pages 24 and 25. Mentors also provide access to privileged (but authorised) information
4 Encouraging exploration of options	See *GROW*, pages 30 and 31
5 Delegating tasks and authority	See *Skill/Will matrix*, pages 54 and 55
6 Effectively confronting negative behaviours	See *Providing Feedback*, pages 24 and 25
7 Providing a role model	Create opportunities for working together, where needed skills can be demonstrated and assimilated

Adapted from *Mentoring* by Gordon Shea

Exercise

Review your performance as a mentor. Compare your perspectives with those of your mentee(s).

Before the sudden arrival of a coach and mentor, the young da Vinci felt that his job was somehow unfulfilling.

The effects of your coaching can be even more powerful than you imagine

20 Reflecting on coaching – a summary

In which Alex recaps his thoughts on coaching

Settling back into his poolside chair, and gazing out over the Aegean once again, Alex came to the end of his career 'flashback'. 'Yes,' he thought, 'but what does the great coach really do, when we cut through all the frameworks?'

Pausing to collect his thoughts, he refilled his glass with ouzo, reapplied the sunscreen and again tapped the recording app.

Let's take a working definition of coaching and then identify the skills and habits which characterise the effective coach. Most coaches have 'grooved' these coaching skills and habits into their daily lives.

Coaching aims to enhance the performance and learning ability of others. It involves providing feedback, but it also uses other techniques such as motivation, effective questioning and consciously matching your management style to each coachee's readiness to undertake a particular task. It is based on helping people to help themselves through interacting dynamically with them – it does not rely on a one-way flow of telling and instructing.

Figure 2 provides a structured list of the activities of the great coach in the workplace. Let's examine them in sequence.

1 Setting the context

This is a critical event; too often we dive into providing feedback with no warning. That can leave the coachee feeling gratuitously 'judged' and unwilling to accept ideas which s/he might otherwise have taken on board.

Figure 2

The coachee's game plan

1 Set the context
   - Diagnose skill and will
   - Agree the approach
   - Build trust
   - Motivate

2 Provide ongoing coaching
   - Use GROW sessions (20–60 minutes)
   - Provide feedback (actionable, frequent, 5–10 minutes)
   - Give praise (frequent, where warranted, 11 minutes)
   - Illustrate actively

3 Conclude effectively
   - Encourage coachee to reflect
   - Elicit feedback for coach
   - Agree next steps

So good coaches habitually make explicit with the coachee the context for their forthcoming interactions. (Figure 3 provides some examples.) However, the coach needs to do some homework first – particularly if s/he is the coachee's boss.

This includes:

- *Diagnosing the skill and will* of the coachee to accomplish the task. Refer back to the Skill/Will matrix on page 55.

- *Agreeing the approach to coaching.* The Skill/Will matrix will suggest the overall coaching approach you will want to take: Directing, Guiding, Exciting or Delegating (pages 55, 126 and 127). However, it is worth being explicit with the coachee about the logistics: How frequently will you provide feedback? What types of coaching sessions will you have? What preparation will you expect of the coachee? You should also make sure you know how your coachees prefer to take in information – by the written word (give them key points in writing), the spoken word (talk to them), visually (illustrate with charts and figures) or by doing (have them work with you in order to practise).

- *Building trust in the coaching relationship.* Effective coaching only really happens when the coachee trusts the coach. This trust may exist from previous interactions you have had with the coachee – or you may need to 'earn' it. A powerful way to do this is to disclose something of your own strengths, weaknesses and experiences. For example, you could share your last performance review with your coachee, or describe relevant situations you have confronted in the past.

- *Motivating the coachee.* Do you know what really motivates the people with whom you work? Try the following exercise: give your colleagues or team mates a copy of pages 128 and 129, amended as you see fit, and share your – and the team's – completed results with them. You will be surprised at the wide variety of responses. Effective motivation requires two things. First, you must know what really excites your coachee about her/his job – why does s/he really come to work in the morning? Second, you will do well to paint an engaging vision of how

Figure 3

Ways to make the context explicit

1   Obtaining coaching

- (To boss) 'I'm really trying to build my skills in [topic]. I'd be very grateful if you could coach me on this, during our next project. Would you be willing to do this? When would it be convenient to discuss the logistics of that coaching support?'

- (To peer) 'I've always thought you were really good at [topic]. I'm trying to get better at this myself. Could I seek your advice and coaching on this during the next few months? Perhaps we could meet for 30 minutes on Friday afternoons/over lunch/over a drink on the occasional evening?'

- (To more junior person) 'I'd really appreciate your feedback and suggestions on [topic]. Even if you think I'm good at this already, I'd appreciate your comments – please don't wait for me to ask.'

2   Providing coaching

- See, particularly, Chapters 5 and 6

well your coachee really could perform, building the cycle of confidence explained on page 67.

2 Providing ongoing guidance

Once the context is understood and agreed, you're ready for a series of coaching interactions. You will already have agreed how often these discussions will take place and how long they will last. In practice, you are likely to use four types of interaction:

- *Substantive sessions of, say, 20 to 60 minutes based on the GROW structure* (refer back to page 30). If your coaching 'contract' extends over two to three months, you may decide to have three such sessions – at the beginning, middle and end of your collaboration. Try to vary the amount of time you spend on the Goals, Reality, Options and Wrap up, to make the most effective use of your time with the coachee.

- *Brief discussions of five to ten minutes, to provide feedback in a timely manner*, soon after the coachee's actions which you have observed.

- *One minute (or longer) sessions of praise* – where warranted. Most coachees do not listen when the typical manager provides positive feedback. Why? Because the coachee is waiting for the inevitable 'but …' which normally follows, and which heralds a series of suggestions for improved performance. By sometimes providing unmitigated praise, you will find your coachee becoming more attentive to your comments and more trusting of you.

- *Active illustration* of how to accomplish the task at which the coachee is trying to build her/his skills. You can accomplish this by demonstration or by collaboration. For example, if you are helping the coachee to run meetings more effectively, you could demonstrate specific points by taking her/him along to one that you yourself are leading. Ask afterwards what s/he observed and what s/he might try differently next time (you could even ask for feedback on your own performance in running that meeting!).

Alternatively, you could collaborate – working with your coachee on a specific task. For example, if the coaching task is to analyse market research data with greater insight, you could work through the detailed data with your coachee so that s/he could see at first hand how insights can be generated.

You can obviously provide these active illustrations only if you yourself are relatively 'expert'. If you lack the necessary expertise in the area in question, you should suggest a 'role model' for the coachee to observe in action.

During these interactions, use the full repertoire of coaching tools which you now know about: the Ask/Tell spectrum (page 9), GROW (page 30), instant payoff coaching (page 49), pure feedback (page 24), motivation (page 66) and others.

3 Concluding the coaching arrangement

You will not want your coaching relationship to just 'fizzle out'. Exactly how you conclude it will depend on factors such as whether your coachee will, in any case, continue working with you or interacting with you socially. However, any conclusion should include at least three steps:

- *Reflection.* Reflection is a critical aspect of how most people learn (see *Educating the Reflective Practitioner* by Schon, cited in the Bibliography). Ensure that the coachee reviews and reflects upon what s/he has learned over the past few months.

- *Feedback to the coach.* Your coachee can probably give you some useful summary feedback on your coaching approach even if s/he has been doing so previously. Make sure you ask for it, and reflect on the experience yourself.

- *Next steps.* Decide whether this is 'goodbye' or 'au revoir'; or perhaps you have been coaching your partner at tennis, and it's time to swap roles.

Alex switched off his recording app, careful to save the file. He got up, stretched, and cast one more glance over the wine dark sea before going over to the one spot that had mobile reception. He dialled his assistant.

'I've been trying to get hold of you all afternoon,' she said, 'the Chairman would like a word with you. Hold on'

Five minutes later he put the phone down, just as his wife was coming in from the pool. 'Sarah, I've got some good news ...'

The 20 golden rules of coaching

Summarising the key lesson from each of the earlier chapters

Appendices

Appendix 1

Coaching (self-) assessment form

Answer the following questions for yourself and/or ask colleagues to complete a copy of this page based on their impressions of you.

How many times in the last week did I ...

1	Provide unconditional praise	☐
2	Give constructive feedback	☐
3	Check a colleague's level of motivation	☐
4	Inspire a colleague	☐
5	Ask for feedback	☐
6	Consciously delegate a task	☐
7	Hold a really effective team meeting	☐
8	Provide upward feedback	☐
9	Check a team's morale	☐
10	'Mentor' a more junior person	☐
	Total	☐

Totals

1–3   If you are not a recluse, you need to study and apply this book carefully

4–6   You can significantly increase your effectiveness at work by applying just a few tips from this book

7–8   You are nearly a master coach

9–10   Give this book to someone who needs it

Priority areas for me to work on

1   _____

2   _____

3   _____

Appendix 2

Feedback plan

Three people to whom I could give useful feedback

1	2	3

Further information I need to gather

When I will provide feedback

Appendix 3

Examples of useful questions when using 'GROW'

Goal

- What is it you would like to discuss?
- What would you like to achieve?
- What would you like from (to achieve in) this session?
- What would need to happen for you to walk away feeling that this time was well spent?
- If I could grant you a wish for this session, what would it be?
- What would you like to be different when you leave this session?
- What would you like to happen that is not happening now, or what would you like not to happen that is happening now?
- What outcome would you like from this session/discussion/ interaction?
- Is that realistic?
- Can we do that in the time we have available?
- Will that be of real value to you?

Reality

- What is happening at the moment?
- How do you know that this is accurate?
- When does this happen?
- How often does this happen? Be precise if possible.
- What effect does this have?
- How have you verified, or would you verify, that that is so?
- What other factors are relevant?
- Who else is relevant?
- What is their perception of the situation?
- What have you tried so far?

Options

- What could you do to change the situation?
- What alternatives are there to that approach?
- Tell me what possibilities for action you see. Do not worry about whether they are realistic at this stage.
- What approach/actions have you seen used, or used yourself, in similar circumstances?
- Who might be able to help?
- Would you like suggestions from me?
- Which options do you like the most?
- What are the benefits and pitfalls of these options?
- Which options are of interest to you?
- Rate from 1–10 your interest level in/the practicality of each of these options.
- Would you like to choose an option to act on?

Wrap up

- What are the next steps?
- Precisely when will you take them?
- What might get in the way?
- Do you need to log the steps in your diary?
- What support do you need?
- How and when will you enlist that support?

Appendix 4

More details on applying the Skill/Will matrix

Direct (skill and will are both low)

- First build the will
  - Provide clear briefing
  - Identify motivations
  - Develop a vision of future performance
- Then build the skill
  - Structure tasks for 'quick wins'
  - Coach and train
- Then sustain the will
  - Provide frequent feedback
  - Praise and nurture
- BUT supervise closely with tight control and clear rules/ deadlines

Guide (low skill, high will)

- Invest time early on
  - Coach and train
  - Answer questions/explain
- Create a risk free environment to allow early 'mistakes'/ learning
- Relax control as progress is shown

Excite (high skill, low will)

- Identify reason for low will – e.g., task/management style/ personal factors
- Motivate (see Chapter 12)
- Monitor, feed back

Delegate (skill and will are both high)

- Provide freedom to do the job
  - Set objective, not method
  - Praise, don't ignore
- Encourage coachee to take responsibility
  - Involve in decision making
  - Use 'You tell me what you think'
- Take appropriate risks
  - Give more stretching tasks
  - Don't over manage

Appendix 5

Motivation exercise – what motivates you most/least

Have members of your team(s) complete copies of these pages and share their results

Factor	Importance of factors*	Current satisfaction*
1 Manager showing concern for you as a person		
2 Having some authority		
3 Good personal relationships with manager		
4 Manager's decisiveness		
5 Examples provided by manager		
6 Being involved in planning your own work		
7 Recognition of your efforts		
8 Delegation of work to you		
9 Being promoted		
10 Customer/client contact		
11 Salary		
12 Extent to which you get on with your peers		
13 Praise		
14 Attaining your own goals and meeting targets		
15 Satisfaction with the job		
16 Working conditions		
17 Having responsibility for discrete areas of work		

*1 = high, 4 = low

Factor	Importance of factors*	Current satisfaction*
18 Working under pressure		
19 A competitive environment		
20 Your prospects of career development		
21 Constructive feedback and coaching		
22 Job security		
23 The result of the completed work		
24 Carrying out complex analysis		
25 The organisation's structure and processes		
26 Your personal job title		
27 Extent of supervision		
28 Social functions		
29 Detailed guidance on how to complete work tasks		
30 Working in a team		
31 Being given clear objectives		
32 Attending high level meetings		
33 Starting work early in the morning		
34 Finishing work late in the evening		
35 Other (specify)		

*1 = high, 4 = low

Appendix 6

Team performance appraisal form

Ask members of your team to complete and discuss copies of this form

Goal		Indicator	Current rating 1 = high, 4 = low
Meaningful purpose	1	All team members feel a common and meaningful sense of purpose behind the project and are clear on its value	
Performance goals	2	The team is working towards achieving agreed goals in an effective manner	
Working approach	3	All team members contribute to the 'real work' on the project, and have a definite and positive role to play	
	4	All team members provide each other with satisfactory real time feedback	
	5	The team operates in a non hierarchical manner (i.e., team members feel that their contributions are fully heard and appraised)	
Complementary skills	6	The team has accessed the right mix of skills, directly and indirectly	
Mutual accountability	7	All team members feel that the achievement of the team goals is recognised and regarded above individual contributions	
	8	Team members provide mutual support and encouragement. Each team member feels accountable for the team's success	
	9	The team is providing opportunities and support to individuals in meeting their goals	
Overall	10	The team has maintained a high level of morale	
	11	All team members have felt strongly motivated throughout this project	

**Suggestions
for improvement**

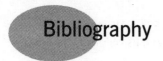

Bibliography

Coaching

Blanchard, K & S Johnson, *The One Minute Manager*, HarperCollins, London, 2001 ● Quick and easy introduction to the basics of coaching and feedback

Bone, D, *Practical Guide to Effective Listening*, Kogan Page, London, 1991 ● A short, comprehensive guide to skills in listening

Buckley, R & J Caple, *One to-One Training & Coaching Skills*, Kogan Page, London, 1991 ● A concise guide to coaching in the business environment

Clutterbuck, D, *Everyone Needs a Mentor*, Chartered Institute of Personnel and Development, London, 5th edition, 2014 ● Helpful guide to thinking through the implications of coaching (mentoring) within your own organisation

Evered, R & J Selman, Coaching & the Art of Management, *Organisational Dynamics* 18 2: 16–32, 1989 ● Short background article on the role of the coach

Gallway, T, *The Inner Game of Golf*, Jonathan Cape, London, 2009
Gallway, T, *The Inner Game of Tennis*, Jonathan Cape, London, 1997
Gallway, T & B Kriegel, *Inner Skiing*, Jonathan Cape, London, 1997
● Introductions to 'coachee- centred' philosophy, principles and questioning techniques using sport

Megginson, D & T Baydell, *A Manager's Guide to Coaching*, British Association for Commercial & Industrial Education, London, 1979 ● A short book about coaching

Mink, O, K Q Owen & B P Mink, *Developing High Performance People: The Art of Coaching*, Addison Wesley Publishing

Company, Reading, Massachusetts, 1993 ● Detailed and painstaking description of coaching and its various applications and techniques

Parsloe, E, *Coaching, Mentoring and Assessing: A Practical Guide to Developing Competence*, Kogan Page, London, 2nd edition, 2009. ● A useful reference for those involved in coaching

Passmore, J, *Psychometrics in coaching: Using psychological and psychometric tools for development*. London: Kogan Page, 2008 ● Covers psychometrics with breadth and depth

Peltier, B, *The psychology of executive coaching: theory and application*. New York, Routledge, 2010 ● Successfully relates coaching to many of the main models of psychology

Rock, D, & L J Page, *Coaching with the brain in mind: Foundations for practice*. Hoboken, N.J: Wiley, 2009 ● Shows how coaching and neuroscience are related

Scoular, A, *The Financial Times guide to business coaching*. Harlow: Financial Times/Prentice Hall, 2011 ● A brilliant guide to coaching in the business environment

Shea, G F, *Mentoring*, Kogan Page, London, 1992 ● Guide to using mentoring as a tool for empowerment

Watkins, M, *The first 90 days: Critical success strategies for new leaders at all levels*. Boston, Mass: Harvard Business School Press, 2003 ● Still the classic text to support role-change

Weinberg, R S & D Gould, *Foundations of Sport and Exercise Psychology* (5th ed.). Champaign, IL: Human Kinetics, 2011 ● A detailed resource for coaches interested in learning from sports coaching

Whitmore, J, *Coaching for Performance: A Practical Guide to Growing Your Own Skills*, Nicholas Brealey, London, 4th edition, 2009 ● Excellent 'self help' guide for the development of coaching skills

Mentoring

Clutterbuck, D, *Everyone Needs a Mentor*, Chartered Institute of Personnel and Development, London, 5th edition, 2014
  ● Helpful guide to thinking through the implications of coaching (mentoring) within your own organisation

Connor, M, & J Pokora, *Coaching and mentoring at work: principles for effective practice*, Maidenhead, Open University Press, 2007
  ● A comprehensive treatment from two dedicated trainers of mentors

Parsloe, E, & M Leedham, M, *Coaching and mentoring: practical conversations to improve learning.* London [u.a.], Kogan Page, 2009 ● A useful reference for those involved in coaching

Shea, G F, *Mentoring*, Kogan Page, London, 1992 ● Guide to using mentoring as a tool for empowerment

Psychology and counselling

Board, R de, *Counselling Skills*, Wildwood House, London, 1987
  ● Down to earth guide on counselling, for the manager

Garfield, C, *Peak Performance*, Warner Books, New York, 1989
  ● Helpful background from sports psychologists about the impact of mental state on performance

Gibb, J R, Trust: *A New View of Personal & Organisational Development*, Guild of Tutors Press, Los Angeles, 1978 ● One of the earliest advocates of Group Development in organisations

Harris, T, *I'm OK, You're OK*, Arrow Books, 2012 ● Outstanding primer on Transactional Analysis, but not as simple as it first appears

Keirsey, D & M Bates, *Please Understand Me: Character & Temperament Types*, Prometheus Nemesis Book Company, Del Mar, California, 1984 ● Introduction to the Myers-Briggs Framework

Whitmore, D, *Psychosynthesis Counselling in Action*, Sage
    Publications Limited, London, 4th edition, 2013 ● Techniques
    and examples of Dr Robert Assagioli's psychosynthesis

Seligman, M E P, *Flourish: A visionary new understanding of happiness
    and well-being*, New York: Free Press, 2011 ● Seligman's latest
    account of positive psychology

Learning

Argyris, C, *Overcoming Organisational Defences: Facilitating
    Organisational Learning*, Allyn & Bacon, Sydney, 1990
    ● Thorough analysis of how social norms and learned
    behaviour can have counterproductive impact on learning and
    communication

Brookfield, S, *Understanding and Facilitating Adult Learning*, Open
    University Press, 2001 ● Introduction to the special challenges
    in helping adults learn new things

Other books on personal development

Bandler, R & J Grindler, *Frogs into Princes*, Eden Grove Editions,
    1990 ● Good introduction to the principles of Neuro Linguistic
    Programming, as applied in daily life

Bennis, W, *On Becoming a Leader*, Basic Books, 2009
    ● An insightful book by a pioneering leader and behavioural
    scientist

Covey, S R, *The Seven Habits of Highly Effective People*, Simon &
    Schuster, London, 25th anniversary edition, 2013 ● A highly
    effective bestseller on how to be more effective

Duhigg, C, *The power of habit: Why we do what we do and how to
    change*, London: William Heinemann, 2012 ● Highly relevant
    since coaching often involves the coachee changing a habit

Hersey, P & K Blanchard, *Situational Leadership: A Summary*,
    University Associates, San Diego, California, 1982 ● One view
    of management development which has had significant impact

Hofstede, G, *Cultures and Organisations*, HarperCollins, London, 3rd edition, 2010 ● Implications of cultures on how we manage and interact

Katzenbach J & D Smith, *The Wisdom of Teams*, McGraw Hill, 2005 ● Advice on the art of building teams and teamwork for high performance

Kolb, D A, *Experiential Learning: Experience as the Source of Learning and Development*. Englewood Clifs: NJ, Prentice-Hall, 1984 ● Learn about learning, from the master of learning

Locke, E A & G P Latham, Building a practically useful theory of goal setting and task motivation, A 35-year odyssey. *The American Psychologist*, 57, 9, 705–17, 2002

Schon, D, *Educating the Reflective Practitioner*, Jossey Bass Publishers, San Francisco, 1987 ● How reflecting on experience can help professionals to learn

Snyder, C R, *The psychology of hope: You can get there from here*. New York: Free Press, 1994 ● Valuable analysis including the distinction between willpower and waypower

Sullivan, W & J Rees, J, *Clean language: Revealing metaphors and opening minds*. Carmarthen, Wales: Crown House, 2008 ● An extreme and valuable version of non-directive coaching

Glossary

AID – see Feedback

Blocks to coaching – A reluctance to coach in certain situations, for reasons which are often misguided. For example the 'control freak' often claims that s/he never has enough time to invest in coaching. This person rarely delegates and becomes caught in a vicious circle of workaholism. There are ways out of these and other predicaments.

Coaching – Coaching aims to enhance the performance and learning ability of others. It involves providing feedback, but it also uses other techniques such as motivation, effective questioning and consciously matching your management style to the coachee's readiness to undertake a particular task. It is based on helping the coachee to help her/himself through interacting dynamically with her/him – it does not rely on a one way flow of telling and instructing.

Delegate (as a management style: see *Skill/Will matrix*) – The preferred approach to managing and coaching people who have high skill and high will to complete the specific task at hand.

Direct (as a management style: see *Skill/Will matrix*) – The preferred approach to managing and coaching people who have low skill and low will to complete the specific task at hand.

Excite (as a management style: see *Skill/Will matrix*) – The preferred approach to managing and coaching people who have high skill but low will to complete the specific task at hand.

Feedback – The process of highlighting to the coachee (a) recent actions, (b) the impact of these actions, and (c), in the broader meaning of the term, desired alternative outcomes where appropriate. Use the acronym AID to remember the three steps (Action, Impact, Desired alternative outcomes).

Goals (a step within *GROW*) – The objectives of the specific coaching session, within the context of the coachee's longer term development objectives.

GROW – A four step structure which helps the coach and coachee to move effectively through a coaching session: Goals, Reality, Options, Wrap up:

- The coach typically uses both 'ask' and 'tell' within each step of the process.
- Clearly, the coach needs to iterate flexibly between the four steps when this is called for.

Guide (as a management style: see *Skill/Will matrix*) – The preferred approach to managing and coaching people who have low skill and high will to complete the specific task at hand.

Instant payoff coaching – A technique for helping someone to resolve a problem in a limited period of time – e.g., 10–15 minutes. The technique focuses on first envisioning what the successful outcome would look or feel like. Subsequent discussion focuses on identifying the source of constraints or blocks to effective action, and how to deal with them.

Mentoring – A role which includes coaching, but also embraces broader counselling and support, such as career counselling, privileged access to information, etc.

Motivation – A critical aspect of managing and coaching – with motivational factors differing widely from individual to individual.

Options (a step within *GROW*) – The brainstormed list of ways in which the coachee can improve her/his performance in a specific area.

Reality (a step within *GROW*) – A description from either the coach – or the coachee her/himself – of what the coachee has done effectively or ineffectively in a recent situation.

Reframing – A process of choosing a different perspective from which to view or address an issue, or a different context within which to consider it.

Skill/Will matrix – A simple way to identify the coach's or manager's appropriate management style, based on the skill and will of the coachee to complete the specific task in question. The four resulting management styles are *Direct*, *Excite*, *Guide* and *Delegate*.

Tao (pronounced 'how' with an initial 'd') – Taoism is a practical philosophy of life which was first codified in China over 2,000 years ago. It maintains that everything is influenced – directly or indirectly – by everything else; that apparent opposites are merely differing manifestations of an underlying unity; and that change is caused by the continuous interplay between yin and yang, as suggested by the familiar symbol ☯. The word 'Tao' means 'the way', in the sense of 'the way in which things happen'.

In terms of coaching, Tao means 'the way in which I work and live in order to derive energy from interacting dynamically with people and things as opposed to expending energy by continually "going against the grain"'.

If yin is 'building the skills and abilities of those who work with us', then yang is 'becoming more effective by delegating to those people whom we have helped to become more able'.

Wrap up (a step within *GROW*) – The coachee's next steps after the coaching session. The plan should be specific, achievable within the agreed timescale, and reflect any assistance needed from third parties.

Acknowledgements

This book grew out of a coaching programme launched throughout McKinsey & Company in the UK during 1990. A previous company version of this guide – written for that programme – therefore benefited from significant input from many of my colleagues across the firm – particularly Sandra Charalambous, Humphrey Cobbold, Kate Grussing, Andrew Glover, Judith Hazlewood, Julian Seaward, Frazer Smith, Kathryn Thomas and Jim Wendler.

Norman Sanson, the firm's UK Managing Director, deserves special acknowledgement. He not only had the vision to launch that initial coaching programme, but also contributed to this book through personal example. I am also indebted to my other partners around the globe for their support.

Ben Cannon – a Director of Alexander – when that coaching firm helped us launch the McKinsey programme – helped bring the book to life, contributing to a number of chapters.

Peter Barnford, Managing Director (Retail) of WH Smith, kindly read through the manuscript and suggested improvements based on his extensive business experience.

I should also like to thank the McKinsey & Company team responsible for the completion of this book: Partha Bose (Director of Communications Europe) provided both incisive comment and strong personal encouragement. Robert Whiting (Publications Editor) and Deborah Thomas (Editor) added continuity to the story and removed anachronism and zeugma. Carole Gardner, Alison Mills and Steph Saul creatively enhanced the book's format.

Finally, I thank HIGGINS (whose cartoons still make me laugh on the twentieth re reading), Martin Liu and Lucinda McNeile (my first two editors); and Andrew Franklin, Penny Daniel and Clare Grist Taylor of Profile Books who shepherded this book through unexpected turns with the greatest of professionalism, and who provided their feedback to the author in the manner of great coaches.

Index